Best Easy Day Hikes Series

Best Easy Day Hikes
Jacksonville, Florida

Johnny Molloy

FALCONGUIDES

GUILFORD, CONNECTICUT
HELENA MONTANA

FALCONGUIDES®

Copyright © 2011 by Rowman & Littlefield

ALL RIGHTS RESERVED. No part of this book may be reproduced or transmitted in any form by any means, electronic or mechanical, including photocopying and recording, or by any information storage and retrieval system, except as may be expressly permitted in writing from the publisher.

FalconGuides is an imprint of Globe Pequot Press.
Falcon, FalconGuides, and Outfit Your Mind are registered trademarks of Rowman & Littlefield.

TOPO! Explorer software and SuperQuad source maps courtesy of National Geographic Maps. For information about TOPO! Explorer, TOPO!, and Nat Geo Maps products, go to www.topo.com or www .natgeomaps.com.

Project editor: David Legere
Layout artist: Kevin Mak
Maps created by Bruce Grubbs © Rowman & Littlefield.

Library of Congress Cataloging-in-Publication Data is available on file.

ISBN 978-0-7627-5295-9

Distributed by NATIONAL BOOK NETWORK

Contents

Acknowledgments

Thanks to all the people who helped me with this book, primarily all the staff at Falcon. Thanks to AyoLane Halusky of the University of North Florida, and to Ken Kennedy for his help. Also, thanks to all the park personnel who tirelessly answered my questions while trying to manage these jewels of the First Coast. The biggest thanks go to the trail builders and hikers of the greater Jacksonville area; without y'all, the trails wouldn't be there in the first place.

About the Author

Johnny Molloy is a writer and adventurer with an economics degree from the University of Tennessee. He has become skilled in a variety of outdoor environments and written over three dozen books, including hiking, camping, paddling, and comprehensive regional guidebooks as well as true outdoor adventure books. Molloy has also written numerous articles for magazines, Web sites, and blogs. He resides in Johnson City, Tennessee, but spends his winters in Florida. For the latest on Molloy's pursuits and work, please visit www.johnnymolloy.com.

Introduction

The boardwalk extends beyond the shore over the St. Johns River. Sitting on a bench, I look westward across the water, toward downtown. The mighty river—the flowing pulse of Jacksonville, with its freshwater tributaries extending inland and tidal tentacles meeting the Atlantic Ocean—flows past the location of many hikes in this book. My mind soars beyond downtown while mentally recounting all the scenic hikes of greater Jacksonville.

Nearby, Jones Creek flows past the wooded trails of the Jacksonville Arboretum. To the east, maritime hammock woods, vast shell mounds, and river views await hikers at Fort Caroline. The protected area of the Talbot Islands contains several trails that wander over ancient wooded dunes, astride tidal creeks bordered by marsh grasses, and even along the Atlantic Ocean. To the north, the green oasis of the Ralph E. Simmons Memorial State Forest protects the woods and paths running beside the St. Mary's River, a magnificent blackwater stream that originates in the Okefenokee Swamp and flows to the sea, where the trails and history of Fort Clinch State Park await hikers.

To the south stands the jewel of Castaway Island Preserve, where boardwalks and nature trails allow hikers to explore a slice of coastal Duval County near popular beaches. Beyond that, the protected wildlands at the University of North Florida offer a five-century-old bald cypress tree, scenic lakes, and a multiplicity of Florida plant and animal communities. To the west, across the St. Johns River, Cary State Forest features a loop trail that cuts into the heart of a swamp hammock, where wetland woodlands regally rise to the sky, encircled by towering pines, with the promise of more trails in the future. The Black Creek Ravines, a conservation project initiated by the St. Johns Water Management District, includes paths that lace its sandhills, richly vegetated ravines, and Black Creek itself. Interpretive information, dark, mysterious creeks, and an ever-changing Florida mosaic of eye-appealing scenery are all part of the trail experience at the vast Jennings State Forest.

With this book in hand and willing feet, you can explore the greater Jacksonville region. No matter where you go, the trails in this book will enhance your outdoor experience and leave you with an appreciation of the natural splendors of the First Coast. Enjoy!

The Nature of Greater Jacksonville

Jacksonville's hiking grounds range from single-track wooded trails along wild streams and salt water to flat and paved park strolls. Hikes in this guide cover the gamut. While by definition a "best easy day hike" is not strenuous and generally poses little danger to the traveler, knowing a few details about the nature of greater Jacksonville will enhance your explorations.

Weather

The climate here is Florida's most temperate, with four distinct seasons. During the long summer highs regularly reach the 90s and a thunderstorm will come most any afternoon. Warm nights stay up in the 70s. Fall brings cooler nights and warm days with less precipitation than summer, and marks the beginning of the hiking season. Winter is variable: Highs push 60 degrees, but expect lows in the 40s, though subfreezing temperatures are the norm during cold snaps. There are usually several mild days during each winter month. Precipitation comes in strong continental fronts, with persistent rains followed by sunny, cold days. The longer days of spring begin the warm-up process, even becoming hot, but temperatures can vary wildly. Heat returns with summer, curtailing the hiking season.

Critters

Jacksonville trail treaders will encounter mostly benign creatures on these trails, such as deer, squirrels, rabbits, wild turkeys, and a variety of songbirds. More rarely seen (during the daylight hours especially) are coyotes, raccoons, and opossums. Deer in some of the parks are remarkably tame and may linger on or close to the trail as you approach. Alligators may be present near water. If you feel uncomfortable when encountering any critter, keep your distance, and they will generally keep theirs.

Be Prepared

Hiking in greater Jacksonville is generally safe. Still, hikers should be prepared, whether they are out for a short stroll at Blue Cypress Park or venturing into the secluded Simmons State Forest. Some specific advice:

- Know the basics of first aid, including how to treat bleeding, bites and stings, and fractures, strains, or sprains. Pack a first-aid kit on each excursion.
- Familiarize yourself with the symptoms of heat exhaustion and heat stroke. Heat exhaustion symptoms include heavy sweating, muscle cramps, headache, dizziness, and fainting. Should you or any of your hiking party exhibit any of these symptoms, cool the victim down immediately by rehydrating and getting him or

her to an air-conditioned location. Cold showers also help reduce body temperature. Heat stroke is much more serious: The victim's skin is hot and dry to the touch, and he or she may lose consciousness. In this event, call 911 immediately.

- Regardless of the weather, your body needs a lot of water while hiking. A full 32-ounce bottle is the minimum for these short hikes, but more is always better. Bring a full water bottle, whether water is available along the trail or not.

- Don't drink from streams, rivers, creeks, or lakes without treating or filtering the water first. Waterways and water bodies may host a variety of contaminants, including giardia, which can cause serious intestinal unrest.

- Prepare for extremes of both heat and cold by dressing in layers.

- Carry a backpack in which you can store extra clothing, ample drinking water and food, and whatever goodies you might want, like guidebooks, cameras, and binoculars. Consider bringing a GPS with tracking capabilities.

- Most Jacksonville trails have cell-phone coverage. Bring your device, but make sure you've turned it off, or keep it on the vibrate setting while hiking. Nothing like a "wake the dead" ring to startle every creature, including fellow hikers.

- Keep children under careful watch. Trails travel along many rivers, streams, lakes, and the ocean, none of which are recommended for swimming. Hazards along some of the trails include poison ivy, uneven footing, and steep drop-offs, so make sure children don't stray from the designated route. Children should carry a plastic whistle; if they become lost, they should stay in one place and blow the whistle to summon help.

Zero Impact

Trails in Jacksonville and neighboring communities are well used year-round, save for the dog days of summer. As trail users, we must be especially vigilant to make sure our passage leaves no lasting mark. Here are some basic guidelines for preserving trails in the region:

- Pack out all your own trash, including biodegradable items like orange peels. You might also pack out garbage left by less-considerate hikers.
- Don't approach or feed any wild creatures—the ground squirrel eyeing your snack food is best able to survive if it remains self-reliant.
- Don't pick wildflowers or gather rocks, antlers, feathers, and other treasures along the trail. Removing these items will only take away from the next hiker's experience.
- Avoid damaging trailside soils and plants by remaining on the established route. This is also a good rule of thumb for avoiding poison ivy and other common regional trailside irritants.
- Be courteous by not making loud noises while hiking.
- Many of these trails are multiuse, which means you'll share them with other hikers, trail runners, mountain bikers, and equestrians. Familiarize yourself with the proper trail etiquette, yielding the trail when appropriate.
- Use outhouses at trailheads or along the trail.

Jacksonville Area Boundaries and Corridors

For the purposes of this guide, best easy day hikes are confined to a one-hour drive from downtown Jacksonville and are primarily in Duval County. Other hikes reach into the counties of Nassau and Clay.

A number of major highways and interstates converge in Jacksonville. Directions to trailheads are given from these arteries. They include I-95, I-295, and SR 9A—the east side of the interstate loop around Jacksonville.

Land Management

The following government organizations manage most of the public lands described in this guide, and can provide further information on these hikes and other trails in their service areas.

- Florida State Parks, Florida Department of Environmental Protection, Division of Recreation and Parks, 3900 Commonwealth Blvd., MS 535, Tallahassee, FL 32399; (850) 245-2157; www.FloridaStateParks.org
- Florida Division of Forestry, 3125 Conner Blvd., Tallahassee, FL 32399-1650; www.fl-dof.com
- Jacksonville Parks & Recreation, 7000 Roosevelt Blvd., Jacksonville, FL 32244; (904) 573-2498; www.coj.net
- Timucuan Ecological and Historic Preserve, 12713 Fort Caroline Rd., Jacksonville, FL 32225; (904) 221-5568; www.nps.gov/timu

How to Use This Guide

This guide is designed to be simple and easy to use. Each hike is described with a map and summary information that delivers the trail's vital statistics, including length, difficulty, fees and permits, park hours, canine compatibility, and trail contacts. Directions to the trailhead are also provided, along with a general description of what you'll see along the way. A detailed route finder (Miles and Directions) sets forth mileages between significant landmarks along the trail.

Hike Selection

This guide describes trails that are accessible to every hiker, whether visiting from out of town or someone lucky enough to live in greater Jacksonville. The hikes are generally no longer than 7 miles round-trip, and most are considerably shorter. They range in difficulty from flat excursions perfect for a family outing to more challenging hilly treks. While these trails are among the best, keep in mind that nearby trails, often in the same park or preserve, may offer options better suited to your needs. I've sought to space hikes throughout the greater Jacksonville region, so wherever your starting point, you'll find a great easy day hike nearby.

Difficulty Ratings

These are all easy hikes, but *easy* is a relative term. To aid in the selection of a hike that suits particular needs and abilities, each is rated easy, moderate, or more challenging. Bear in mind that even the most challenging routes can be made easy by hiking within your limits and taking rests when you need them.

- **Easy** hikes are generally short and flat, taking no longer than an hour to complete.

- **Moderate** hikes involve increased distance and relatively mild changes in elevation, and will take one to two hours to complete.

- **More challenging** hikes feature some steep stretches, greater distances, and generally take longer than two hours to complete.

These are completely subjective ratings; consider that what you think is easy is entirely dependent on your level of fitness and the adequacy of your gear (primarily shoes). If you are hiking with a group, you should select a hike with a rating that's appropriate for the least-fit and -prepared person in your party.

Approximate hiking times are based on the assumption that on flat ground, most walkers average 2 miles per hour. Adjust that rate according to the steepness of the terrain and your level of fitness (subtract time if you're an aerobic animal, and add time if you're hiking with kids), and you'll have a ballpark hiking duration. Be sure to add more time if you plan to picnic or take part in other activities, like bird-watching or photography.

Trail Finder

Best Hikes for River and Stream Lovers

Best Hikes for Children

Best Hikes for Dogs

Best Hikes for Great Views

Best Hikes for Boardwalks

Best Hikes for History Buffs

Best Hikes for Nature Lovers

Map Legend

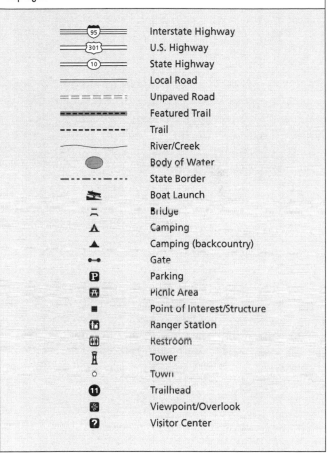

══○95══	Interstate Highway
──○301──	U.S. Highway
──○10──	State Highway
────────	Local Road
═ ═ ═ ═ ═	Unpaved Road
▬▬▬▬▬▬▬	Featured Trail
- - - - - - -	Trail
～～～～	River/Creek
⬭	Body of Water
─ ∙ ─ ∙ ─ ∙	State Border
🛥	Boat Launch
⌒	Bridge
⛺	Camping
▲	Camping (backcountry)
•—•	Gate
🅿	Parking
⛩	Picnic Area
■	Point of Interest/Structure
🏠	Ranger Station
🚻	Restroom
🗼	Tower
○	Town
⑪	Trailhead
🖼	Viewpoint/Overlook
❓	Visitor Center

1 White Sand Landing Loop

This lengthy trek travels the heart of Ralph E. Simmons State Forest, making a side trip to White Sand Landing, on the banks of the scenic St. Mary's River. Leave the river, passing through myriad natural communities, which increase your chances for seeing wildlife. Backpackers take note that two backcountry campsites lie along the route.

Distance: 7.2-mile loop
Approximate hiking time: 3.5 to 4 hours
Difficulty: More challenging due to distance
Trail surface: Natural surfaces
Best season: Oct through Apr
Other trail users: Equestrians
Canine compatibility: Leashed dogs permitted

Fees and permits: No fees or permits required
Schedule: Sunrise to sunset
Maps: Ralph E. Simmons Trailwalker Trails, USGS Boulogne
Trail contacts: Ralph E. Simmons State Forest, 3742 Clint Dr., Hilliard, FL 32046; (904) 845-3597; www.fl-dof.com

Finding the trailhead: From exit 28A, New Kings Road, on I-295 near Jacksonville, take US 1 north to Callahan. From the intersection of US 1 and SR A1A in Callahan, continue north for 17.8 miles to Lake Hampton Road, just before the US 1 bridge over the St. Mary's River. Ignore signs for Ralph E. Simmons State Forest until you reach Lake Hampton Road. Turn right on Lake Hampton Road and follow it for 2.5 miles to Penny Haddock Road. Turn left on Penny Haddock Road and follow it for 0.8 mile, then veer left into the trailhead parking area. GPS Trailhead Coordinates: N30° 47' 38.5", W81° 56' 18.4"

The Hike

This is the longest hike in this guidebook. It offers a chance to not only test your physical skills but also to explore the remote heart of the Ralph E. Simmons State Forest, and perhaps to see wildlife scattered amid the numerous plant ecosystems in the St. Mary's River valley near the Georgia border. The loop, known as the White Trail, is marked with white diamond blazes as it joins and loses old forest roads. However, where these roads meet or divide, the correct route is clearly marked with the blazes, so don't be afraid of getting lost. If you go some distance without seeing a white blaze, then back up. Do expect to hear the afternoon wind pushing through the trees, and perhaps a deer rustling away in an oak thicket, or an armadillo digging at the soil.

The forest continually changes character, from open pine flatwoods to crowded swamp hardwoods, thick with ferns and cane, especially in the bottoms closer to the river. The two campsites located along the St. Mary's River off the main loop are first come, first served, and are accessible only by foot or boat. The St. Mary's is a fine paddling river. Do not bypass the spur trail to White Sand Landing, a riverside beach and campsite shaded by live oaks. Somebody with a good arm—and a rock—could throw a stone to Georgia from there.

The White Trail leaves the trailhead and high ground and aims for the St. Mary's River. It comes within 0.25 mile of the river and then turns north and runs roughly parallel with the St. Mary's. You can see the river before angling south back toward the trailhead. In most places swamp woods divide the trail from river. An aura of seclusion accompanies you throughout the hike. Hunting is allowed

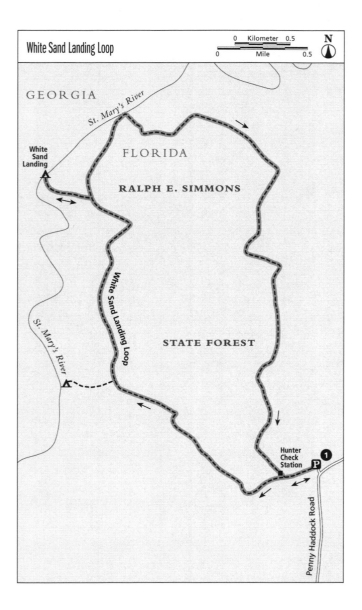

in the state forest, so make sure and check ahead of time for hunt dates at http://myfwc.com.

Miles and Directions

0.0   Pass around a gate near the trailhead kiosk, traveling westerly on a double-track of sand and plant fodder. Turkey oaks and pine shade the path.

0.1   Reach a hunter check station. Here the path divides. Stay left with the white blazes, now on a narrower track.

0.4   Reach a sand fire road junction in longleaf pines. Stay right with white blazes, heading northwesterly.

1.0   Stay left at an intersection, downhill into moist woodland.

1.5   A spur trail leads left to a campsite, the first of two on the St. Mary's River. The spur trail is marked with a small blue sign with a tent symbol on it. The White Trail passes through row-cropped pines.

1.6   Bridge a swamp stream strand by culvert. Note the tupelo and cypress trees growing in the streambed.

2.4   Reach a "T" intersection. Here, the White Trail turns left with the white blazes and heads almost due west.

2.7   An elevated spur trail leads left through swamp hardwoods to White Sand Landing and a campsite. Take this spur trail and the opportunity to see the St. Mary's River.

3.0   Make White Sand Landing. Live oaks tower over a flat sloping to a sand beach and an exemplary blackwater river.

3.3   Head north on the White Trail in lush woods after returning from White Sand Landing.

3.8   The White Trail comes within sight of open water on the St. Mary's, then turns away on a relatively faint track.

4.3   Watch for an unexpected left turn marked with white blazes. Bisect a hardwood swamp of red maple, tupelo, and widely buttressed pines.

4.7   The White Trail crosses a closed forest road. Keep straight.

5.0 Reach a "T" intersection. Stay right with the White Trail.

5.5 Head left, easterly, on an elevated road berm through seasonally inundated forest.

5.8 Head right at a trail junction, now walking southbound.

6.4 Turn left at an intersection to bridge a streamlet. Ascend on a gullied track into row-cropped pines.

6.9 Reach a major double-track sand road. Turn left toward the hunter check station.

7.1 Reach the hunter check station. Begin backtracking.

7.2 Arrive back at the trailhead.

2 St. Mary's River Loop

This hike explores the Ralph E. Simmons State Forest, rolling through mixed woodland before descending to the St. Mary's River, where a sandy river access allows good views of the river dividing Florida from Georgia. Travel along the river corridor. Your return route climbs from the river bottom and then loops back to the trailhead.

Distance: 3.3-mile loop
Approximate hiking time: 1.5 to 2.5 hours
Difficulty: Moderate
Trail surface: Natural surfaces, gravel
Best season: Oct through Apr
Other trail users: Equestrians
Canine compatibility: Leashed dogs permitted

Fees and permits: No fees or permits required
Schedule: Sunrise to sunset
Maps: Ralph E. Simmons Trailwalker Trails, USGS Boulogne
Trail contacts: Ralph E. Simmons State Forest, 3742 Clint Dr., Hilliard, FL 32046; (904) 845-3597; www.fl-dof.com

---

Finding the trailhead: From exit 28A, New Kings Road, on I-295 near Jacksonville, take US 1 north to Callahan. From the intersection of US 1 and SR A1A in Callahan, continue north for 17.8 miles to Lake Hampton Road, just before the US 1 bridge over the St. Mary's. Ignore signs for Ralph E. Simmons State Forest until you reach Lake Hampton Road. Turn right on Lake Hampton Road and follow it for 1.6 miles to the trailhead on your left, just beyond a set of power lines. GPS Trailhead Coordinates: N30° 46' 47.2", W81° 57' 11.0"

The Hike

This hike travels through the southern portion of the Ralph E. Simmons State Forest, a 3,700-acre swath of land stretching along the St. Mary's River in Nassau County. Interestingly, this forest has within its bounds the most northerly parcel of the Sunshine State. Throughout its length, the St. Mary's River forms the boundary line between Florida and Georgia. The forest is located within a northerly bend of the St. Mary's. The land was purchased using Preservation 2000 and Save Our Rivers funds. Hunting is allowed in the forest, so check http://myfwc.com for hunt dates before hitting the trail.

Using a combination of two loop trails, the Yellow Trail and the Red Trail, this adventure wanders through a forest mosaic which changes as elevation and situation changes. One minute you will be traveling through turkey oaks and palmetto patches, and the next minute you will be underneath pine groves. Oak forest rises astride the St. Mary's. The trail itself is used as a dividing line in prescribed fire management. The result is sometimes differing types of forest habitats on either side of the trail you are following.

The route, primarily a double-track path with a natural duff and sand composition, is marked with yellow and red diamond blazes nailed to trees as it works downhill to the St. Mary's, where you briefly join a power line. Here, the blackwater stream is tidally influenced, rising and lowering, but salt water never makes it this far upriver. Freshwater trees border the flow, primarily cypress. At low tides small sand beaches are exposed in places along the river.

The path then travels downstream along the river corridor atop a bluff where you can look through the trees into Georgia. After your views of the Peach State, the loop curves toward the trailhead. Pay attention as the vegetation changes with elevation, from swamp to mixed woodland to longleaf pines with an understory of wiregrass. The remainder of the hike is an easy stroll through eye-appealing forest.

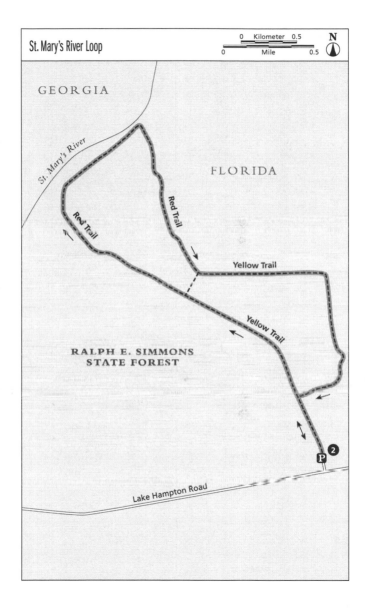

St. Mary's River Loop

0   Kilometer   0.5
0   Mile   0.5

N

GEORGIA

St. Mary's River

FLORIDA

Red Trail

Red Trail

Yellow Trail

Yellow Trail

RALPH E. SIMMONS
STATE FOREST

P   2

Lake Hampton Road

Miles and Directions

0.0   Leave the fenced trailhead parking area and kiosk, heading north around a road gate. Enter an area of young planted longleaf pines on the Yellow Trail. Shortly enter natural forest.

0.2   Reach a junction. Your return route comes in from the right. Keep straight, tracing the yellow blazes on a slight descent, shaded by laurel oak and pine.

0.8   Reach another trail junction. Here, the Yellow Trail turns right to make a 1.8-mile loop. However, this hike keeps forward, now joining the Red Trail. The descent sharpens as you travel northwesterly for the St. Mary's River.

1.0   Reach a power line in a marshy area. The trail stays on an elevated berm under the power line.

1.3   Meet the St. Mary's River. The power line clearing affords access to the sand-bordered waterway. The Red Trail leaves the power lines and turns northeast, roughly paralleling the St. Mary's River in dense woodland of wax myrtle, palmetto, sand live oaks, and sweetgums. Sun-exposed parts of the trail are sandy. Enjoy views from a wooded bluff.

1.6   Reach a river access, then turn away from St. Mary's, traversing a wooded wetland of tupelo and cypress.

1.7   Rise to higher ground in mixed woodland.

2.1   Level off in classic longleaf/wiregrass forest complemented with turkey oaks.

2.2   The Red Trail ends. Keep straight, rejoining the Yellow Trail, now curving easterly through a level open forest, making for easy hiking.

2.6   The Yellow Trail turns sharply right, southbound.

3.0   After curving west, the trail passes a St. Johns River Water Management District monitoring station.

3.1   The Yellow Trail completes its loop. Turn left here, backtracking.

3.3   Reach the trailhead.

3 Cary Trailwalker Trail

This loop takes you through pine forest into the middle of a wooded swamp on an elevated boardwalk with a top-down view of wetlands. The boardwalk offers a dry-footed examination of an otherwise inaccessible ecosystem. The trek, used by school groups on field trips, then travels a grassy road to span more wetlands before returning to pine flatwoods and looping back to the trailhead.

Distance: 1.3-mile loop

Approximate hiking time: 0.5 to 1 hour

Difficulty: Easy

Trail surface: Natural surfaces, boardwalk

Best season: Oct through Apr

Other trail users: None

Canine compatibility: Leashed dogs permitted

Fees and permits: Recreation fee required

Schedule: Sunrise to sunset

Maps: Cary Sale Forest, Cary Trailwalker Trail, USGS Bryceville

Trail contacts: Cary State Forest, 7465 Pavilion Dr., Bryceville, FL 32209; (904) 266-5021; www.fl-dof.com

Finding the trailhead: From exit 343 on I-10 west of downtown Jacksonville, take US 301 north for 1 mile, then veer right into the town of Baldwin on Beaver Street / US 90 / US 301. Travel for 0.6 miles east through the town, then turn left, staying with US 301, and follow it for 7.1 more miles to Pavilion Road and Cary State Forest. Turn right on Pavilion Road and follow it for 0.3 mile to the trailhead near a picnic area and kiosk at the intersection with Fire Tower Road. The trail starts on the west side of Pavilion Road. GPS Trailhead Coordinates: N30° 23' 59.63", W81° 55' 35.99"

The Hike

Bring a picnic with you and enjoy a meal at the trailhead. You also have the option of camping here, as three campsites—complete with warm showers and restrooms—are located near the trailhead. Cary State Forest is located west of downtown Jacksonville near the town of Bryceville. The state forest straddles the Nassau/Duval county line. The original tract was one of the first state forests in Florida. It now has been expanded to 7,355 acres. More trails and camping opportunities are slated for the future, using the added tract. Check with the division of forestry for supplemental hiking opportunities. This particular hike takes place in the westernmost part of the forest in a designated safety zone (i.e., no hunting allowed); therefore, hikers can enjoy this trail every day of the year.

The trail leaves the picnic area to enter longleaf pines with a brushy understory. The building you soon reach is the state forest teaching pavilion, used primarily for school groups. Interpretive information is scattered along the designated footpath bordered by fetterbush and yaupon, with a pine-needle-and-grass footbed about 5 feet wide. The natural surface soon gives way to the Adams Wilderness Boardwalk, named for a couple that donated funds to construct the boardwalk. The wooden walkway allows you to enter a hardwood hammock without damaging the vegetation—or getting your feet wet and muddy.

Notice the buttressed trees. Since the moist soil can't hold these swamp trees very well, the base of their trunks and lowermost roots spread outward to keep from tipping over. Cypress trees are easy to spot with their "knees." The function of these woody protrusions is still not known to botanists. It was once thought these knees allowed often-inundated cypresses to "breathe."

Sweetbay magnolia is another common tree in the swamp. It is a tall evergreen with a gray trunk that prefers the wetter margins of forests. Sweetbay's long elliptical leaves have a silvery white underside that make it easy to identify. It is common in wetlands throughout Florida.

The boardwalk winds through the hammock, then briefly joins a sandy forest road before reentering the woods as a footpath. Meander through woodlands before returning to the teaching pavilion and restroom building. Since this is a relatively short hike, you can also walk a second boardwalk by stepping a few feet south from the intersection of Fire Tower Road and Pavilion Road and by picking up the wooden walkway, then heading easterly. By the way, the state forest fire tower, within sight of the trailhead, is open to the public. The view from there is worth the climb.

Miles and Directions

0.0 From the trailhead kiosk walk north across Pavilion Road. Look for a sign that reads NATURE TRAIL / TEACHING PAVILION. Enter longleaf flatwoods, reaching the Teaching Pavilion, a multisided wood structure. Turn right here, heading northeast.

0.3 A spur path leads right toward the park office and outbuildings.

0.4 Reach a resting bench and the beginning of the boardwalk.

0.5 Leave the boardwalk to join Moccasin Slough Road, a sandy double-track closed to vehicles. Turn left here.

0.7 Hogtrap Road leaves right. The trail stays left on Moccasin Slough Road, then turns left into the woods as a footpath. Wander through pines.

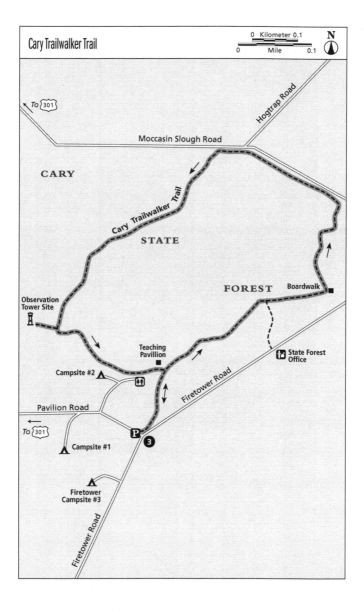

1.1 Reach a "T" junction. A short spur trail travels right to the side of an old observation tower. Head left, then emerge near the restroom building. The Teaching Pavilion is within sight. Backtrack toward the picnic area and trailhead.

1.3 Arrive back at the trailhead.

4 Camp Milton Preserve Walk

Walk a series of nature trails through what was once a Confederate fort. Now you can enjoy not only the area history but also its natural beauty along McGirts Creek. It's easy to extend your hike here, as Camp Milton Preserve serves as the primary trailhead for the Jacksonville-Baldwin Rail Trail.

Distance: 1.9 miles
Approximate hiking time: 1.2 to 2 hours
Difficulty: Easy
Trail surface: Poured concrete
Best season: Oct through Apr
Other trail users: None
Canine compatibility: Leashed dogs permitted
Fees and permits: No fees or permits required
Schedule: 9 a.m. to 5 p.m.
Maps: Camp Milton, USGS Marietta
Trail contacts: Camp Milton Preserve, 1175 Halsema Rd. South, Jacksonville, FL 32221; (904) 630-3586; www.campmilton.com

Finding the trailhead: From exit 351 on I-10 west of downtown Jacksonville, take Chaffee Road north for 0.2 miles to US 90 / Beaver Road. Turn left on US 90 west / Beaver Road and follow it 1.2 miles to Halsema Road. Turn right on Halsema Road and follow it 1.5 miles to the preserve, on your right. GPS Trailhead Coordinates: N30° 20' 3.93", W81° 52' 7.78"

The Hike

The Confederate Army established a fort in 1864 and was stationed here, trying to lure Union troops out of Jacksonville while simultaneously protecting the food pipeline running north from the cattle country of Central Florida to Rebel troops. Today, the site has not only been preserved but also enhanced with interpretive trails that explain the historic area. You can also enjoy heritage trees that are planted along the paths. These heritage trees are spliced from historic originals relevant to the Civil War. For example, a sycamore tree comes from General Robert E. Lee's family estate in Virginia. Another comes from the site of Lincoln's tomb on the Capitol Mall. Another comes from Jacksonville's very own Treaty Oak.

You can also travel over McGirts Creek on a recreated Civil War bridge. The Harvey homestead site gives you an idea of what farm life was like in the 1860s. And there is a final perk: Camp Milton Preserve is the main trailhead and midpoint for the Jacksonville-Baldwin Rail Trail. This 14-mile asphalt path stretches both directions from here, allowing you to extend your hike until your legs wear out. Or perhaps you'd prefer to hike the preserve trails and then jump on your bicycle for a ride on the rail trail. No matter how you do it, come and give this well-maintained, attractive preserve a chance.

It's hard to get up a hiking head of steam at Camp Milton because the plethora of interpretive signage is too interesting to ignore. You can always stroll around the fort preserve and then burn calories on the rail trail. From the trailhead, the Earthworks Trail will take you through open fields and into a gorgeous hardwood hammock. It then circles around earthworks left over from the fort, where 8,000 Southerners were stationed. Named for Florida governor John Milton, the fort extended beyond the boundaries of the preserve south along Halsema Road.

The hike then passes the Harvey homestead to cross a replica bridge over McGirts Creek. From there, meet the Jacksonville-Baldwin Rail Trail. Here's your opportunity to add mileage to the hike. Otherwise, backtrack toward the

Camp Milton Preserve Walk

0   Kilometer   0.1
0   Mile   0.1

N

Jacksonville–Baldwin Rail Trail

McGirts Creek

Rail Trail Connector

American Forest Trail

Replica Bridge

Learning Center

Harvey Homestead

Halsema Road Sidewalk

Trail Road

4

P

Earthworks Trail

Halsema Road

Old Plank Road

trailhead and pick up the American Forest Trail, where you can see an abundance of heritage trees brought here from all over the South—places like the Shiloh Battlefield in Tennessee and the Andersonville Military Prison in Georgia. Learn about the Civil War while appreciating the beauty of these shade-bearing plants.

The rail trail came to be through the efforts of several government agencies. Initially, the city of Jacksonville bought the 14.5 miles of unused CSX Railroad line in 1992. Over time, the Florida Department of Greenways and Trails has gotten involved, and the trail is now an asset for Jacksonville, with Camp Milton as the centerpiece.

Miles and Directions

0.0 With your back to Halsema Road, take the double-track trail, Trail Road, lined with live oaks, easterly.

0.1 Reach a trail junction. Turn right on the Earthworks Trail. Travel through a field, then join a boardwalk through wetland woods, rife with ferns and vines.

0.4 The boardwalk splits. Begin looping around old Confederate earthworks, now thickly forested. Two boardwalk spurs extend toward Old Plank Road.

0.6 Complete the boardwalk loop and then backtrack to Trail Road.

1.0 Turn right on the Trail Road, shortly passing the Harvey homestead and the Learning Center and Historic Museum.

1.2 Cross the re-created Civil War bridge over McGirts Creek. Backtrack, then stay right, joining the Rail Trail Connector.

1.5 Meet the Jacksonville-Baldwin Rail Trail. The asphalt track travels east-west for many a mile. This hike backtracks to pick up the American Forest Trail.

1.9 Reach the trailhead.

5 Fire & Water Nature Trail

This hilly interpretive trail in the Jennings State Forest takes you through numerous plant communities and to informative stops that explain the importance of fire and water for Florida's forests. Enjoy a wildlife blind and an overlook above Wheeler Branch, a blackwater stream, and perhaps see some insect-eating pitcher plants.

Distance: 1.8-mile loop
Approximate hiking time: 1 to 1.5 hours
Difficulty: Moderate due to hills
Trail surface: Natural surfaces
Best season: Oct through Apr
Other trail users: None
Canine compatibility: Leashed dogs permitted

Fees and permits: Recreation fee required
Schedule: Sunrise to sunset
Maps: Fire & Water Nature Trail, Jennings State Forest USGS Fiftone
Trail contacts: Jennings State Forest, 1337 Long Horn Rd., Middleburg, FL 32068; (904) 291-5330; www.fl-dof.com

Finding the trailhead: From exit 12 on I-295 southwest of downtown, take Blanding Boulevard (SR 21) south for 8 miles to Old Jennings Road. Turn right onto Old Jennings Road and follow it for 4.1 miles nearly to a dead end, then turn right on Live Oak Road, a sand road. Follow it for 1.5 miles to reach the trailhead on your left (at 0.5 mile, you will pass the trailhead for the North Fork Black Creek Trail). GPS Trailhead Coordinates: N30° 8' 11.26", W81° 52' 55.67"

The Hike

Jennings State Forest stretches across 23,000 acres of fast-growing northern Clay County as well as a portion of Duval

County, near the town of Middleburg. Centered on North Fork Black Creek, the forest provides recreational opportunities for visitors and a place for wildlife to call home. Land managers are anxious to restore this area to preserve the natural communities vital to northeast Florida's long-term vigor. The Fire & Water Nature Trail takes you through many of the ecosystems found in the state forest. Accompanying interpretive information explains the importance of fire and water to the landscape. Be aware that hunting is allowed in the forest, so check ahead of time for hunt dates.

Live oaks shade picnic tables at the trailhead and make for an attractive pre- or post-dining spot. The hike begins amid a sandhill forest. These forests, comprised primarily of longleaf pines with wiregrass understory, were heavily logged a century ago. Without proper fire management, along with changeover from natural forest to urbanized uses, the longleaf/wiregrass habitat has been greatly reduced, along with plant and animal species that call it home. Therefore, the Jennings State Forest serves as an important natural oasis in greater Jacksonville.

The path is marked with painted blazes and is easy to follow. Work the margin between the sandhill forest and thickly wooded wetlands, composed primarily of bay trees and known as a *baygall*. The primary trees in this habitat are the sweetbay magnolia (the largest), along with understory trees, the loblolly bay and red bay. Following the beginning loop portion of the hike, a spur trail leads right to a wildlife blind. If you decide to take the spur trail to the blind, be quiet; plant yourself between the wooden fences cut with narrow sight lines; and be patient! If you are still and quiet and give it some time, you may see some critters of the state forest. Likely candidates are deer, turkeys, and armadillos.

Fire & Water Nature Trail

Live Oak Road

Wildlife Blind

Sweetwater Lane

JENNINGS

STATE

FOREST

Observation Deck

Wheeler Branch

Sweetwater Lane

N

0 Kilometer 0.1

0 Mile 0.1

5

Birders may get lucky. Did I say you need to be quiet and patient? I have seen deer here myself.

The loop continues northwesterly toward Wheeler Branch. Note the longleaf pines making a comeback with proper fire management. Pass a seepage slope and an opportunity to see some pitcher plants, still traveling the border of sandhill and thicker, wetter woodland. The path curves southerly as it joins a hill dropping to Wheeler Branch. Grab a view from an observation deck into the steeply sloped stream valley, where serpentine Wheeler Branch flows under Southern magnolias. Repose benches beckon. Travel along the stream.

The trek climbs away from Wheeler Branch only to drop and span one of its tributaries. This feeder branch flows steeply off the sandhills and spills noisily under the bridge, adding audio appeal to your walk. The path makes an easterly track primarily in pines, but does cross the head of that tributary one more time. Wander through eye-appealing woods and then backtrack after completing the loop portion of your hike.

Miles and Directions

- **0.0** Leave the trailhead, walking around a pole gate, passing a kiosk, which should have the interpretive handout for the Fire & Water Nature Trail. Join a wide track bordered by turkey oaks and pines with scattered palmetto.

- **0.2** The trail splits. Begin the loop portion of the hike. Stay right so you can follow the numbered interpretive stops. Bisect a thickly wooded wetland.

- **0.3** Take a spur trail leading right under mixed forest to the wildlife blind. Backtrack to the main loop.

- **0.6** Curve around a seepage slope with a colony of pitcher plants nearby.

0.9 Reach an observation deck extending toward Wheeler Branch. Look down on the precipitous wooded slope to the sand-bottomed blackwater streamlet.

1.1 Make a sharp right turn and descend to bridge a tributary of Wheeler Branch. Travel easterly along the line between the stream woods to your left and pines to your right.

1.4 Step over the head of a seepage slope, bordered by cane.

1.6 Complete the loop portion of the hike. Turn right here and backtrack toward the trailhead.

1.8 Reach the trailhead.

6 North Fork Black Creek Loop

This excellent day hike—with backpacking possibilities—explores the hills, woods, and streams of Jennings State Forest. First, travel along and across Sweetwater Branch before reaching the brooding North Fork Black Creek and a campsite. Your return trip takes you over rolling terrain and through pine flatwoods. Hikers making this loop early or late in the day stand a good chance of seeing wildlife.

Distance: 5.2-mile loop
Approximate hiking time: 2.5 to 3.5 hours
Difficulty: More challenging due to length
Trail surface: Natural surfaces
Best season: Oct through Apr
Other trail users: None
Canine compatibility: Leashed dogs permitted

Fees and permits: Recreation fee required
Schedule: Sunrise to sunset
Maps: Jennings State Forest Trailwalker Trails, USGS Fiftone
Trail contacts: Jennings State Forest, 1337 Long Horn Rd., Middleburg, FL 32068; (904) 291-5330; www.fl-dof.com

Finding the trailhead: From exit 12 on I-295 southwest of downtown, take Blanding Boulevard (SR 21) south for 8 miles to Old Jennings Road. Turn right onto Old Jennings Road and follow it for 4.1 miles nearly to a dead end, then turn right on Live Oak Road, a sand road. Follow it for 0.5 mile to reach the Old Jennings trailhead on your left. GPS Trailhead Coordinates: N30° 7' 20.8", W81° 52' 56.5"

The Hike

This hike has a lot to offer, starting at the trailhead with its attractive picnic area, picnic shelter, and restrooms, perched on the eastern edge of the 23,000-acre Jennings State Forest. From there, hike to the lush centerpiece of the preserve—North Fork Black Creek, where a campsite awaits. Your return route travels through high pinelands where a sense of remoteness is very real. Be aware that hunting is allowed in the forest, so check ahead of time for hunt dates.

The trail system is well marked and maintained, keeping you literally on track, focusing on your surroundings rather than trying to figure out where you are. Though the trailhead is shared with equestrians, the North Fork Black Creek Trail is for hikers only, except for a few short distances where it shares treadway with the Evans Horse Loop. The hike's beginning has several trail intersections with short loops and the horse trail. Things settle down as it runs the margin between sandhill woods and swamp forest along Sweetwater Branch.

Throughout the hike the forest composition is continually changing—from open pine flatwoods to live-oak / turkey oak strands to cypress and bay strands to streamside slope forests. This woodland mosaic creates an ever-changing panorama that is a feast for the eyes. Vertical variation, aka, hills, has much to do with this. The sandhills of the Jennings State Forest easily drain, creating a drier landscape up top while sending water to the bottoms below, where the added water creates a verdant landscape.

Walk along Sweetwater Branch, running into the horse trail a couple more times, and travel through wet bottomland forest. Aim for North Fork Black Creek, a dark brooding blackwater stream ensconced in a junglesque riot of vegetation. The spur trail to the backcountry campsite and the stream itself is your ticket to this wooded netherworld, which makes for a great relaxation spot. Note the canoe/

kayak landing along the waterway and Sweetwater Branch coming in just upstream of the landing.

Your return trip from the North Fork takes you into pine country. The open sky can bake the path here, making for loose sand and slow going on the now-level path. Make the trailhead after a couple of junctions at loop's end.

Miles and Directions

0.0 From the north side of the Old Jennings trailhead parking area, near the trailhead kiosk, look for the sign heading right, easterly, indicating North Fork Black Creek Trail. The Evans Horse Loop heads left, westerly. The trail leads you to Live Oak Road, then turns north along a fence line running parallel to Live Oak Road.

0.1 Leave the fence line, entering a mixed forest of live oak, palmetto, and pine.

0.3 Reach a trail junction. Here, a spur trail leads right to a wildlife-viewing blind. The Bird Blind Loop heads left and this hike keeps straight, running in conjunction with the Longleaf Loop. Traverse pine/palmetto woods with the slope of Sweetwater Branch to your right.

0.6 Intersect the Evans Horse Loop. The horse and hiking trail run in conjunction.

0.8 Come to a four-way trail junction. The Longleaf Loop heads left. The Evans Horse Loop keeps straight and this hike turns right, diving into rich, thick woods toward Sweetwater Branch. Shortly bridge the sand-bottomed stream in swamp woods, then climb into turkey oak forest. Travel west along the margin where the ecosystems merge. Listen for Sweetwater Branch gurgling over roots as it falls toward North Fork Black Creek, and to frogs croaking in the adjacent wetland.

1.0 Keep straight as the horse trail crosses.

1.2 Step over a seep flowing toward Sweetwater Branch.

North Fork Black Creek Loop

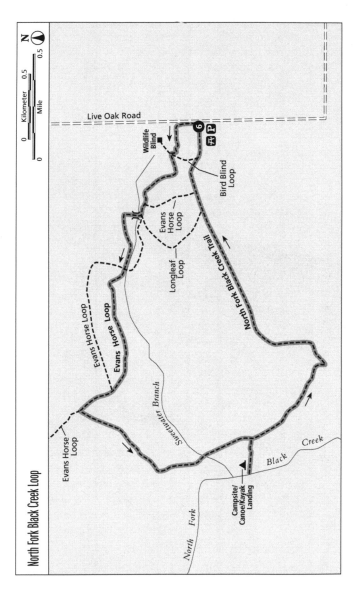

1.7 Intersect the horse trail again. The hiking trail and horse trail run in conjunction for the next 0.2 mile.

1.9 The North Fork Black Creek leaves left as the horse trail keeps straight. Enter thick wooded wetland dominated by red maple. The trail could be muddy or partially submerged here.

2.6 Cross Sweetwater Branch.

2.9 Join the spur trail leading right to North Fork Black Creek and a designated backcountry campsite.

3.0 Reach the backcountry camp, complete with picnic tables and tent pads. Continue beyond the campsite toward North Fork Black Creek, descending to reach the stream and a canoe/kayak landing near a limestone outcrop. Backtrack and rejoin the loop southbound.

3.7 Turn left away from North Fork, now heading easterly.

4.0 Step over a seep and then ascend into widely spaced pines and turkey oaks. Stay with the blazes and you'll encounter a few sand roads, heading northeast for the trailhead.

4.8 The narrow Longleaf Loop comes in from your left. Keep straight with the blazes.

4.9 The Evans Horse Loop comes in on your left. Keep straight as the two trails run in conjunction, now entering pine flatwoods.

5.0 The narrow Bird Blind Loop comes in on your left. Keep straight.

5.2 Complete the loop, reaching the Old Jennings trailhead.

7 Black Creek Ravines Hike

This trek travels through a protected swath of lower Black Creek. Here, make a double loop in hilly terrain, passing sensitive seepage slopes and making Black Creek, where you can enjoy views of the waterway from an oak bluff. The final part of the hike passes two ravine observation points, allowing a good look into this increasingly rare natural community.

Distance: 4.4-mile double loop

Approximate hiking time: 2 to 3 hours

Difficulty: Moderate due to hills and distance

Trail surface: Natural surfaces

Best season: Oct through Apr

Other trail users: Equestrians

Canine compatibility: Leashed dogs permitted

Fees and permits: No fees or permits required

Schedule: Sunrise to sunset

Maps: Black Creek Ravines Conservation Area, USGS Middleburg

Trail contacts: St. Johns River Water Management District, 4049 Reid St., Palatka, FL 32178; (386) 329-1429; www.sjrwmd.com

Finding the trailhead: From exit 12 on I-295 southwest of downtown, take Blanding Boulevard (SR 21) south for 13 miles to Clay County Road 218 on the south side of Middleburg. Turn left on CR 218 east and follow it for 2 miles; then turn left on Green Road. Follow Green Road for 0.8 mile to the trailhead on your right. Note: You will see an initial trailhead at 0.6 mile under some power lines; this is alternate parking. The better parking and primary trailhead is at 0.8 mile. GPS Trailhead Coordinates: N30° 3' 29.0", W81° 50' 48.3"

The Hike

We are fortunate that St. Johns River Water Management decided to purchase and preserve this scenic tract just outside of Middleburg. Here, Black Creek is making a major bend around steep sandhills. Drainages cut ravines in the sandhills leading to Black Creek. Elevations range from 90 feet at its highest point to 5 feet above sea level at Black Creek. The draining of the high sandhills has created deep wooded ravines and seepage slopes, which are uncommon communities and thus are protected by the conservation area.

Furthermore, the 973-acre tract also functions as a water recharge area for Black Creek and the greater St. Johns River. Over 2.7 miles of water frontage on Black Creek are kept in a natural state. Part of this hike travels along the south shore of Black Creek, and a spur trail leads from the loop to a backcountry campsite located on conservation area property.

There are a total of three loops at Black Creek Ravines and they are blazed in white, yellow, and red. As a whole the trail system is well marked and maintained. It uses a combination of single-track and double-track paths. In some places, since equestrians also ply the trails, the trail track will be looser.

The hike itself explores the conservation area through two connected loops. Travel through mixed pine and oak woods, heading northbound. Make a trail junction and an alternate loop hike extends to the east side of the property. Our loop, however, continues north, skirting a seepage slope. It then begins its second loop, passing under a power line before reaching Black Creek. Here you can gain a bluff-top view of the alluring dark stream, which is quite wide at this point.

Travel along the shoreline, gaining more views before climbing the path away from the water. The second half of the hike provides the best vantages of the ravines for which the conservation area is named. Here the path travels along the edge of the sandhills and the drop-off into the ravines. Two designated observation points allow you to safely peer down into the surprisingly steep plant communities, which contrast greatly with the sandhills up top. The narrow ravines allow more shade, and the increased moisture creates luxuriant plant communities. But it's not all about plants; you may also see deer, gopher, tortoises, and bird life here at the ravines.

Miles and Directions

0.0 From the parking area, join the single-track White Trail as it enters rich oak woodland.

0.2 Make a trail junction. This is the beginning of the actual White Trail loop. Stay right, heading northeast. A group campsite and restroom are visible off to your left. The level track belies nearby ravines.

0.6 Reach a trail junction in oaks. Here, the Red Trail makes a separate 2.5-mile loop. Stay left with the White Trail, heading north.

0.9 Intersect the Yellow Trail. The White Trail heads left and will be your return route. Keep straight on a downgrade and skirt the edge of a seep. Briefly open onto a power line before returning to woods.

1.5 Reach the loop portion of the Yellow Trail. Turn right here, heading to the east side of the power lines and meet the Yellow Spur. Turn left and follow the road heading north under the easternmost power lines, passing astride a hard-

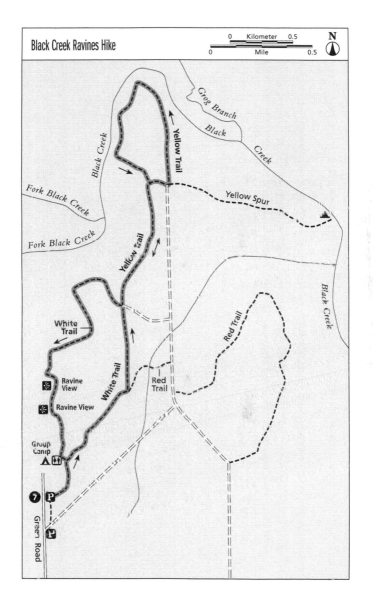

Black Creek Ravines Hike

wood swamp on either side of the power lines. The Yellow Spur goes easterly 0.7 mile to a backcountry campsite along Black Creek.

2.1 Come alongside the shoreline of Black Creek. Make a bluff-top cruise above the cypress-lined shoreline.

2.3 Leave the waterway, passing through moist oak woods before climbing.

2.5 Complete the Yellow Trail loop. Begin backtracking, still on the Yellow Trail.

3.1 Meet the White Trail. This time turn right, walking the margin between sandhill and seepage slope.

3.8 Come to the first ravine observation point.

3.9 Reach the second ravine observation point.

4.1 Complete the White Trail loop near the group campsite and restroom. Stay left and backtrack toward the trailhead.

4.4 Reach the trailhead.

8 Ortega Stream Valley Trail

This trail leads through verdant oak woodland and is located at Ringhaver Park, operated by the city of Jacksonville. The thick, shady forest allows year-round hiking. Reach a spur trail where an elevated boardwalk avails a top-down view of a freshwater hardwood swamp before reaching a dock on the Ortega River. Enjoy the aquatic aspect of the trek before returning to the trailhead.

Distance: 1.6-mile balloon loop
Approximate hiking time: 1 to 1.5 hours
Difficulty: Easy
Trail surface: Asphalt
Best season: Year-round
Other trail users: None
Canine compatibility: Leashed dogs permitted

Fees and permits: No fees or permits required
Schedule: 7:30 a.m. to dusk
Maps: None; USGS Orange Park
Trail contacts: Ringhaver Park, 5198 118th St., Jacksonville, FL 32244; (904) 630-2489; www .coj.net

Finding the trailhead: From exit 16 on I-295 southwest of downtown, take SR 134 east for 1 mile to a red light and Blanding Boulevard (SR 21). Turn right on SR 21 and follow it for 1 mile to 118th Street. Turn left on 118th Street and follow it east for 1.4 miles to Ringhaver Park, on your right. Follow the main park road 0.3 mile to the trailhead parking just before the tennis courts. GPS Trailhead Coordinates: N30° 13' 45.33", W81° 42' 57.04"

The Hike

Ringhaver Park, run by the city of Jacksonville, is a large multipurpose facility, seemingly with a little something for everyone—including hikers. It offers tennis courts, playgrounds, ball fields, and picnic facilities, all situated on the west bank of the Ortega River, a stream starting in far western Duval County. Though much of the park is developed, a large swath of hardwood swamp and woodland close to the Ortega River remains in a natural state.

The Ortega Stream Trail travels through a portion of this natural area, offering undeveloped beauty to complement the developed park facilities. However, after coming here you will wish the trail system was expanded to include more of the natural area. If you desire a longer hike, then simply walk the trail a couple of times or more, as is done by the many regulars who use this path for their daily exercise. In addition to hikers, paddlers also use the trail to access the canoe/kayak launch located on the Ortega River, so don't be surprised if you see someone carrying a boat on the hiking trail!

A small shady gazebo marks the trail's beginning. Thick woods with an overstory of pine are complemented by bountiful oaks and maple. Dense undergrowth and dangling vines indicate that it's been a long time since these fire-dependent woods have burned. Since Ringhaver is an urban park bordered on three sides by residences, it is unlikely that fire will be used to maintain the natural character of the woods; thus, it is likely they will remain thick and completely convert to an oak-dominated hardwood forest.

A wetter part of the woodland through which the trail passes is dominated by bay trees—sweetbay magnolia and red bay. A few areas are open and sandy, while other spots have regal live oaks towering overhead. You'll also notice a few sand trails that spur on and off the asphalt loop. If you stay with the asphalt, you can't get lost. Make sure and take the 1,000-foot boardwalk to the Ortega River—it's the highlight of the hike.

Maples, sweetgums, and other hardwoods form the nucleus of the swamp. Late fall is a good time to walk the boardwalk and see these trees in their autumn finery. Spring is also a good time to visit and see the colorful buds before they transform into green leaves. Consider bringing binoculars as the boardwalk is also a good birding location; since it's situated near the water, you can view shorebirds, but it's also in the swamp, where the elevated perch will increase your chances of seeing songbirds.

Since this part of the Ortega River is tidally influenced, the floating dock is designed to rise and lower with the tides, yet it will allow you easy access to the water no matter the tidal time. This is where paddlers launch, floating out from the inlet in front of you to explore the main river. Consider bringing a watercraft of your own and doubling your fun here at Ringhaver Park.

Miles and Directions

0.0 Pick up the asphalt path leaving south from a small gazebo next to the parking area. Shortly curve behind the tennis courts, entering thick woods.

0.2 Reach a boardwalk over wetland forest. Just ahead a spur trail leads right, connecting to a neighborhood on Morse Avenue. The Ortega Stream Valley Trail continues on another boardwalk.

0.3 Reach the loop portion of the hike. Keep forward here as your return route comes in on the left. Pass through a live-oak copse.

0.5 The loop curves back to the north after reaching the south end of the park.

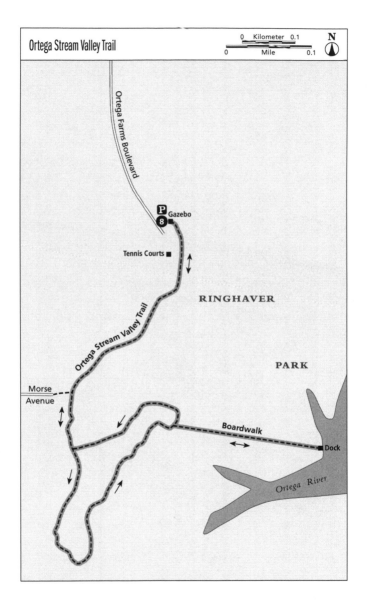

Ortega Stream Valley Trail

0   Kilometer   0.1

0   Mile   0.1

N

Ortega Farms Boulevard

P 8 Gazebo

Tennis Courts ■

RINGHAVER

Ortega Stream Valley Trail

PARK

Morse
Avenue

Boardwalk

Dock

Ortega River

0.8 Reach a trail junction. Turn right. Here, an asphalt path soon reaches the elevated boardwalk. Climb the wooden walkway and enjoy your perch as you travel easterly through a hardwood swamp. The boardwalk ends at a dock. Enjoy watery views of the Ortega River. Backtrack.

1.2 Continue the primary loop, traveling through more oaks.

1.3 Complete the loop. Backtrack toward the trailhead.

1.6 Finish the hike.

⑨ Blue Cypress Park Hike

This Jacksonville city park hike takes you along the shores of the St. Johns River and out to a pier with a great view of downtown Jacksonville and beyond. It also loops into a towering maritime hammock rife with live oaks. The first part of the hike travels among developed facilities at this multipurpose preserve.

Distance: 2.4-mile double loop
Approximate hiking time: 1 to 2 hours
Difficulty: Easy
Trail surface: Asphalt and natural surfaces
Best season: Oct through Apr
Other trail users: None
Canine compatibility: Leashed dogs permitted

Fees and permits: No fees or permits required
Schedule: Sunrise to sunset
Maps: None; USGS Arlington, Eastport
Trail contacts: Blue Cypress Park, 4012 University Blvd. North, Jacksonville, FL 32202; (904) 630-2489; www.coj.net

Finding the trailhead: From the Merrill Road / Jacksonville University exit on SR 9A northeast of downtown, take Merrill Road west for 2.8 miles to University Boulevard. Turn right on University Boulevard and follow it for 1.7 miles to Blue Cypress Park, on your left. After entering the park, pass the clubhouse, and then park where the gravel fishing pier access road leaves left, just beyond the park pool. GPS Trailhead Coordinates: N30° 22' 29.4", W81° 36' 35.1"

The Hike

Once known primarily for its golf course, Blue Cypress Park has since been transformed into more of a multipurpose facility, with an added emphasis on its natural features. In fact, the former eighteen-hole course was reduced to nine holes. Originally part of the Edenfield Estates housing development, the environmentally sensitive and scenic 118-acre tract was purchased by the city. It is set on the eastern bank of the St. Johns River, north of downtown, on land that would go for astronomical prices these days, for its river views alone.

Most of the urban shoreline of greater Jacksonville has been developed, yet this park offers an unspoiled stretch where you not only can travel out to a pier over the river, but also hike a boardwalk that runs along the St. Johns. In addition, you can access the grass shoreline, punctuated with small beach areas from breaks in the boardwalk. A gorgeous live-oak hardwood hammock rises away from the river, and this hike makes a loop through the heart of it. The asphalt trail is 6 to 8 feet wide in the developed part of the park. Exercise stations, with pull up bars and such, have been periodically set up along the path. The undeveloped part of the park utilizes natural surfaces, but be careful: The trail segment in the live-oak hammock is somewhat rooty, so watch your footing.

The beginning of the hike makes a loop near the developed facilities—a park inspection tour, if you will. Along the way you'll pass a pool and the old golf clubhouse—now a community center; you'll also pass a lake, playground, soccer fields, and tennis courts. The trail then heads west away from the developed facilities and cruises through some of the remaining golf course before reaching the fishing pier and boardwalk. Span a tidal creek bordered by marsh grasses. This is a good birding area. The flow of the water

Blue Cypress Park Hike

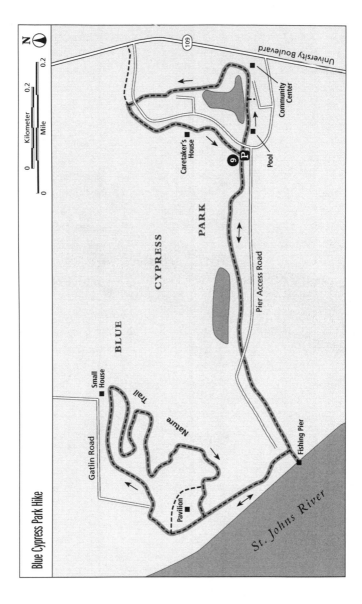

in the tidal creek will reveal whether the tide is coming in or going out. Scattered pines and cedars gain purchase in the sandy soil.

Upon leaving the St. Johns, the path enters a maritime hammock complete with palms, Southern magnolia, sweet-bay magnolia, and live oaks draped in Spanish moss, forming a green cathedral. The now-natural-surface path snakes throughout the hammock, making the most of the available terrain, then emerges along the open St. Johns River shoreline where you can gain one last view before backtracking to the trailhead.

Miles and Directions

0.0 From the intersection of the park road and the spur gravel road leading to the fishing pier, take the asphalt path heading easterly toward University Boulevard. Immediately pass the swimming pool and begin circling around the park lake, passing the old clubhouse, now a community center. Ahead, the path takes you by a play area and tennis courts.

0.2 Cross the park road and reach a trail junction. Here a short asphalt path leads right to University Boulevard. This hike leads left and goes near the park caretaker's house.

0.6 Complete the loop, returning near the trailhead parking area. Continue following the asphalt path, now heading westerly into a thick forest with especially tall trees. The woods give way to a grassy field astride the golf course.

0.8 Cross the fishing pier access road after passing a small pond. Continue west, aiming for the St. Johns River.

0.9 Reach the fishing pier and boardwalk. Head out to the pier, enjoying first-rate views of the St. Johns River, port facilities, and downtown Jacksonville. A small gazebo shades the pier's end. Now, walk north on the boardwalk running parallel with the St. Johns River.

1.2 A spur trail leads right to a covered pavilion. This will be your return route. The boardwalk soon gives way, allowing easy access to the shoreline. At lower tides small sand beaches will be exposed. Shortly pass a second spur trail leading right toward the pavilion.

1.3 Reach an alternate parking area accessed from Gatlin Road. You are now in a maritime hardwood hammock. The trail begins winding through the lush woods, circling near a small house.

2.0 Emerge at the pavilion near the St. Johns River. Travel toward the St. Johns and then pick up the boardwalk and begin backtracking.

2.4 Complete the hike.

10 Jacksonville Arboretum and Gardens

A fine trail system has been developed on this 120-acre tract along Jones Creek. The paths takes advantage of the terrain, exploring wooded ravines, blackwater stream bottoms, an old excavation pond, and some incredible live oaks scattered in hilly woodland. Expect more from this natural preserve in the future.

Distance: 1.6-mile triple loop
Approximate hiking time: 1 to 1.5 hours
Difficulty: Easy
Trail surface: Natural surfaces, a little pavement
Best season: Year-round
Other trail users: None
Canine compatibility: Leashed dogs permitted

Fees and permits: No fees or permits required
Schedule: 8 a.m. to 5 p.m.
Maps: Jacksonville Arboretum, USGS Arlington
Trail contacts: Jacksonville Arboretum and Gardens, P.O. Box 5763, Jacksonville, FL 32247; www.jacksonvillearboretum.org

Finding the trailhead: From the Monument Road exit on SR 9A east of downtown, take Monument Road east for 0.1 mile to Millcoe Road. Turn left on Millcoe Road and follow it 0.2 mile to the right turn into the Arboretum parking area. GPS Trailhead Coordinates. N30° 20' 46.22", W81° 32' 22.69"

The Hike

The site of the Arboretum, located near SR 9A, has been through many incarnations before becoming one of Jacksonville's up-and-coming natural preserves. At one time a railroad line ran through the property. Later, what was to become Lake Ray was the site of a mining operation, probably a phosphate mine. The land was purchased for a park in the 1970s but was not developed. The land was allowed to recover, obliterating many signs of the past. The lake created by the mining operation became an asset. The Arboretum's grand opening was held in 2009, and things are only going to improve with time. Currently a parking area and trail comprise the Arboretum infrastructure.

The master plan calls for a research facility, native plant garden, visitor center, and many more trails. Future paths will explore the multiplicity of environments here, from maple wetlands to tidal marshlands to sand ridges. Board-walks will traverse swamps. A trail will be dedicated to exploring the history of the citrus railroad that traversed the property. Watching this park grow is going to be exciting. You can contribute to this project financially, with your time, or in many other ways. Visit the Arboretum's Web site to help make this preserve a showcase of Jacksonville outdoors.

The current trail system is a good start, and those who come here and hike will certainly be inspired by the possibil-ities at the arboretum. There is a drawback, however—road noise from SR 9A. Wooden posts mark the well-maintained paths. Interpretive information is scattered throughout the preserve. The forest here has an everywhere-you-look beauty no matter what segment of the trail system you are hiking. The Ravine Trail rides a hilltop looking down on a desiccated spring run flowing below. These hills contrast with the Jones Creek bottoms, a junglesque riot of growth bordering dark waters.

Travel along the stream in hilly terrain before coming to Lake Ray. Once a mining operation, the impoundment makes for a very alluring body of water. Ringed with trees and scattered with surface vegetation, the pond is set in a small valley bordered by hills. Any clearings you may see are the result of an aggressive exotic plant eradication campaign. Part of the mission of the Arboretum is to eradicate invasive species while simultaneously protecting the existing biological diversity of northeast Florida.

Beyond Lake Ray, the hike enters a live-oak hammock and wanders the margin between the swamp woods of Jones Creek and hillside scrub oaks. However, plenty of large live oaks reign over these woods. You will find some cut stones for sitting, where the Live Oak Trail and the Lake Loop meet. The hill provides a good vantage for relaxing and looking down on Lake Ray. One final trek on the Lake Trail leads you back to the trailhead.

Miles and Directions

0.0 From the main trailhead and kiosk, facing east, join the red-blazed, natural-surface Ravine Trail as it circles past a retention pond, then passes a sabal palm hammock. Ignore the paved beginning of the Lake Loop. Enter full-blown woods after crossing the head of a ravine on a short wooden bridge. Turn easterly, running parallel with the spring runs toward Jones Creek.

0.2 Intersect the Jones Creek Trail. The Ravine Trail heads left to bridge the spring runs. This hike turns right on the Jones Creek Trail to bridge a channel of Jones Creek, crossing an island before bridging a second channel of Jones Creek.

0.4 Bridge Jones Creek again, then shortly meet a spur trail leading right to the Lake Loop. Turn right on the Lake Loop and begin circling Lake Ray.

Jacksonville Arboretum and Gardens

0.6 Meet the Live Oak Trail. Turn right here, entering deep woods. Watch for some distinctive live oaks with incredibly widespread arms, including one tree with a palmetto bush growing in the crooks of its arms. Resurrection ferns cover many a live-oak limb here.

1.1 Complete the Live Oak Trail and meet the Lake Loop. It is but a short distance back to the trailhead right, but go left, circling Lake Ray and making a hill climb before finishing the hike.

1.6 Arrive back at the trailhead.

11 Hammock Trail at Fort Caroline

This hike at Fort Caroline National Monument explores a hilly maritime forest before dropping to the St. Johns River and the site of a French bastion from the 1500s. Enjoy not only the human history but also the natural beauty of this shoreline. Give yourself ample time to not only hike the trail, but also to explore the fort and stop in at the visitor center.

Distance: 1.2-mile loop
Approximate hiking time. 1 to 1.5 hours
Difficulty: Easy, but has hills
Trail surface: Natural surfaces
Best season: Oct through Apr
Other trail users: None
Canine compatibility: Leashed dogs permitted
Fees and permits: No fees or permits required
Schedule: 9 a.m. to 5 p.m.
Maps: Fort Caroline Official Map & Guide, USGS Mayport, Eastport
Trail contacts: Timucuan Ecological and Historic Preserve, 12713 Fort Caroline Rd., Jacksonville, FL 32225; (904) 641-7155; www .nps.gov/timu

Finding the trailhead: From the Monument Road exit on SR 9A east of downtown, take Monument Road east for 4 miles to meet Fort Caroline Road. Turn right on Fort Caroline Road and follow it for 0.1 mile, then turn left, staying with Fort Caroline Road, as Mount Pleasant Road heads straight. Next, turn left toward the Fort Caroline visitor center and reach the trailhead / visitor center parking area. GPS Trailhead Coordinates: N30° 23' 8.41", W81° 29' 52.12"

The Hike

Fort Caroline National Memorial is part of the greater Timucuan Ecological and Historic Preserve, a sizable agglomeration of tidal waters and lands northeast of downtown Jacksonville. Run by the National Park Service, Fort Caroline preserves the approximate spot where French explorers established a colony in 1564. The original intent of the colony was to find riches such as those the Spaniards were bringing home from elsewhere in the New World, but it ended up having a religion factor as well, since the French Protestants, known as Huguenots, were being persecuted in France.

The colonists tried to carve out a living along the shores of the St. Johns but found the going tough in America. Though occupied by the Timucuan Indians, who were alternately friend and foe to the Huguenots, the lands were nevertheless claimed by the Spaniards, who attacked Fort Caroline in 1565, slaughtering most of the inhabitants before occupying the fort themselves. The French recaptured Fort Caroline but didn't attempt to colonize the area any further. Unfortunately, there are no remains of the actual fort itself, which may have been obliterated during the dredging of the St. Johns River. However, the approximate location is believed to be correct.

Today you can learn about the life ways of the colonists and the Timucuan Indians and about the greater ecological preserve at this visitor center, as well as hike the Hammock Trail, which wanders through a gorgeous maritime hammock forest. Travel over ancient shell mounds and dunes that give the hike some serious vertical variation. The Hammock Trail is a natural-surface path about 4 feet wide. The park service keeps this trail and the grounds of Fort Caroline shipshape, making for an eye-pleasing experience with no bad surprises. Contemplation benches await those willing to relax and absorb the atmosphere. Over two dozen interpretive information stops are stretched out along the loop, turning this hike into a human and natural history learning experience. The hike is described below in a clockwise direction, allowing you to save Fort Caroline and the St. Johns River for last.

Enter live-oak-dominated woodland where Spanish moss hangs on anything that doesn't move. Other oaks, huge pines, hickory, Southern magnolia, sweetgum, wax myrtle, cedar, and still more trees comprise the high-canopied forest undulating over ancient sand dunes. After rolling through the hilly woods, the path wanders into marsh, bridging a tidal stream, which adds to the biodiversity of the hike. The hike leads to the Fort Caroline replica located along the St. Johns River, where you can walk among the earthworks, guns, and walls of the moat encircled fort, imagining what it would be like to live here along the wide waterway. Take note of the huge pines near the fort. Several short nature paths give you various options to choose from on your return trip from the fort to the visitor center. Watch for the replica Timucuan hut on your way back.

Miles and Directions

0.0 As you face the visitor center, look left for the signed Hammock Trail trailhead. Shortly join a 4-foot-wide natural-surface path heading toward Fort Caroline, walking but a few feet to reach another trail junction. Here, a narrow connector trail leads left and downhill to join the actual Hammock Trail. Stay left with the Hammock Trail, heading south.

0.3 The loop makes a turn to the right, now heading southwest.

0.4 Top out on a hill after a solid climb. Begin descending to a gate, then turn right again, walking north for Fort Caroline and the St. Johns River.

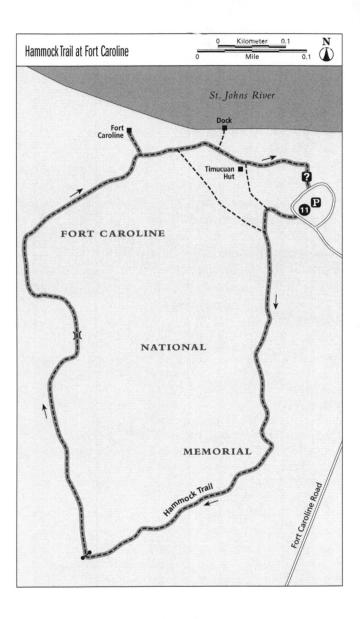

Hammock Trail at Fort Caroline

St. Johns River

Dock

Fort Caroline

Timucuan Hut

?

11 P

FORT CAROLINE

NATIONAL

MEMORIAL

Hammock Trail

Fort Caroline Road

N

0   Kilometer   0.1

0   Mile   0.1

0.7 Bridge a marshy tidal stream.

1.0 Emerge at the Fort Caroline replica. The original fort has been lost to time, but what you see now is a physical rendering using the maps and notes of Jacques Le Moyne, an artist and mapmaker who lived at the colony. Keep east on a wide trail, staying left, closest to the river, as a trail leads right back to the parking area.

1.1 Reach a spur trail leading left to a dock on the St. Johns.

1.2 Reach the visitor center, completing the hike.

12 Spanish Pond Loop

One of Jacksonville's finest day hikes, this trek travels over wooded ancient dunes of a maritime hammock onto even hillier Timucuan shell mounds, past a hermit's cabin, to an observation point overlooking a salt marsh along the St. Johns. Your return trip passes a Confederate soldier's grave and then reaches a high point and vista before returning to the trailhead.

Distance: 2.9-mile balloon loop
Approximate hiking time: 2 to 2.5 hours
Difficulty: Moderate due to hills
Trail surface: Natural surfaces
Best season: Oct through Apr
Other trail users: None
Canine compatibility: Leashed dogs permitted

Fees and permits: No fees or permits required
Schedule: 9 a.m. to 5 p.m.
Maps: Fort Caroline Official Map & Guide, USGS Mayport
Trail contacts: Timucuan Ecological and Historic Preserve, 12713 Fort Caroline Rd., Jacksonville, FL 32225; (904) 641-7155; www .nps.gov/timu

Finding the trailhead: From the Monument Road exit on SR 9A east of downtown, take Monument Road east for 4 miles to meet Fort Caroline Road. Turn right on Fort Caroline Road and follow it for 0.1 mile, then turn left, staying with Fort Caroline Road, as Mount Pleasant Road heads straight. Next, turn left toward the Fort Caroline visitor center and instead of turning left into the visitor center, turn right to the Fort Caroline picnic area. GPS Trailhead Coordinates: N30° 23' 3.0", W81° 29' 44.7"

The Hike

The Theodore Roosevelt Area of the Timucuan Ecological and Historic Preserve covers 600 acres of maritime hammock, salt marshes, and incredible shell mounds, deposited by the Timucuan Indians. A quality trail system has been integrated into the tract. The beauty of the area was recognized by a man named Willie Browne, who resided here nearly all his born days before turning his land over to the Nature Conservancy so it could be left in its natural state and enjoyed by others.

This hike travels by Browne's cabin site, a small clearing in the forest. Just a few moments at his retreat will persuade you to see his point of view. Browne's arrival at this spot was accidental, a simple twist of fate. Early in the 1900s Browne's parents moved to Jacksonville from New York City. They had settled down in Florida when a yellow fever epidemic swept across Jacksonville; they came out to this land near Fort Caroline to escape the disease. Willie and his brother Saxon grew to love life in their neck of the woods, and fashioned a living through fishing, timbering, and more. Browne saw the vast urbanization around him and couldn't bear the thought of this spot being turned into condos. Fortunately, it didn't happen, and Browne lived more than eighty years before passing away.

The hike begins on the Spanish Pond Trail, aiming for the observation tower on the marshes of the St. Johns. The heavily wooded path first circles by its namesake body of water, a good birding area mostly screened by vegetation. As is the case here in Florida, the slightest elevation changes alter the forest composition. Pines and palmettos occupy their place on higher ground, but the junglesque maritime hammock of live oak, Southern magnolia, palms, and cedars are most common. Ancient sand dunes and shell mounds lend vertical variation. Sand live oaks find their place on the hills.

Take time to repose at Willie Browne's cabin site before heading out to a strand of land and the wooden observation tower. Higher tides may inundate part of the path. At the tower, you can look out on the salt marsh of the St. Johns River and back toward the wooded shell mounds the Timucuans called home for thousands of years.

Your return route travels the Timucuan Trail; by climbing a ridge of shells atop the marsh, you will enjoy great views of the marsh and beyond. Don't miss the grave of Confederate soldier Sergeant John Nathan Spearing.

Miles and Directions

0.0 Leave the shaded parking area on the red-blazed Spanish Pond Trail and immediately join a boardwalk that leads to a natural-surface trail. Head right, as the trail going left accesses another part of the parking area.

0.1 Reach another of many boardwalks over part-time wetlands. Where the boardwalk isn't present, the maritime hammock in these bottoms will have a rooty track. Watch your feet while also enjoying the immense beauty of the area.

0.8 Meet the Timucuan Trail coming in from your left. This will be your return route. For now, stay right, descending from a hill, still on the red-blazed Spanish Pond Trail. The track shortly widens.

1.0 Come to a four-way junction. Here, the Willie Browne Trail comes in from the right. The trail going left shortcuts over to the Timucuan Trail. Keep straight, still on the Spanish Pond Trail.

1.1 Climb a hill and reach the Willie Browne cabin site and another trail junction. Here, another arm of the Willie Brown Trail leaves right to an alternate parking area off Mount Pleasant Road. A single-track path leaves left to the Timucuan Trail. Keep forward toward the observation tower.

1.3 Reach and climb the observation tower after passing the Timucuan Trail and traveling a slender cedar-covered spit. Backtrack, then join the Timucuan Trail.

1.4 Pass the grave of Confederate soldier, Sergeant John Nathan Spearing. A spur trail leads left, back to the Browne cabin site.

1.5 An alternate path leads to the Willie Browne Trail. Keep climbing.

1.8 Come to a high point and view of the Timucuan lands below. Your best views are to the north. Drop off the hill on a sandy track in scrubby oaks.

2.1 Meet the Spanish Pond Trail. Turn right and backtrack.

2.9 Reach the trailhead, completing the hike.

13 UNF Nature Trails

This loop hike takes place on the University of North Florida campus at the Sawmill Slough Preserve. The hike uses several trails in a complex that travels through multiple habitats, including maple and cypress swamps, passing by an ancient cypress tree, and around Lake Oneida.

Distance: 3.0-mile loop
Approximate hiking time: 2 to 2.5 hours
Difficulty: Moderate
Trail surface: Natural surfaces and boardwalks
Best season: Oct through Apr
Other trail users: None
Canine compatibility: Dogs not allowed

Fees and permits: Parking fee required Monday through Friday; weekends and holidays are free
Schedule: Sunrise to sunset
Maps: Robert W. Loftin Nature Trails, USGS Arlington
Trail contacts: UNF Department of Recreation, 1 UNF Dr., Jacksonville, FL 32224; (904) 620-1810; www.unf.edu/recsports

Finding the trailhead: From the University of North Florida exit east of downtown on SR 9A, take UNF Drive east for 0.5 mile to turn right into UNF parking lot 100. Immediately purchase a parking pass at the drive-through window, then park. GPS Trailhead Coordinates: N30° 15' 55.7", W81° 30' 39.7"

The Hike

Back in 1973, the University of North Florida came together to build some hiking trails in the wilds of Sawmill Slough. Led by Robert Loftin, to whom the trail system is dedicated, these trails on approximately 500 acres of UNF property were opened to the public, including the very first wheelchair-accessible path in greater Jacksonville. Before the decade was out this trail system was federally recognized as a National Recreation Trail, a big acknowledgment in the trail world. Over time this trail system has been altered, expanded, and otherwise improved. In 2006 the university officially preserved this campus wildland in perpetuity, to be used for recreation, education, and research. It is also a state-protected bird sanctuary. This area deserves preservation, as it offers a variety of habitats, including open lake, hardwood swamp, pine flatwoods, sandhill forests, and seepage slopes. Today you can explore these communities using multiple trails and loops. Be apprised there is a drawback—car noise from SR 9A and SR 202.

The trailhead has a fine picnic area, restrooms, and designated parking. Make sure and buy a parking pass if you are here on a weekday! The university operates nature programs for students and school groups from the area. Enrolled UNF students have the advantage of being able to check out canoes and kayaks to paddle Lake Oneida.

The university continues to improve the landscape, attempting to restore it to its natural state using prescribed fires and elimination of invasive species. The part of Sawmill Slough north of UNF Drive is off limits to visitors and is used for research purposes only. This particular hike explores the southern part of the slough and adjacent lands, starting on the preserve's longest path—the Goldenrod Trail. Exercise stations are located periodically along the path. Interpretive information enhances the trek. Pines, maples, palms, and oaks shade the trail and ground palmetto. Your hike shortly leaves left on the Big Cypress Loop. Here you can view a five-century-old bald cypress that survived the logger's ax. The reason: When you look at the tree, its trunk is divided a short ways up; that's because two trees have grown together, resulting in a wood density too tough for the saws of bygone days.

The loop continues, entering a maple swamp before curving back north and coming along a man-made lake dug for fill to elevate a nearby SR 9A interchange. The hike picks up a sandhill ridge cloaked in pines, which contrasts with Sawmill Slough, a lush hardwood swamp which you cross before meeting Lake Oneida. Circle around Lake Oneida, completing the hike. If you are looking for more trails to trek, travel the Red Maple Boardwalk as it makes a loop in wetlands near the lake.

Miles and Directions

0.0 After parking, walk toward the exit of parking lot 100. Look for the yellow-blazed Goldenrod Trail leaving south from the parking area. Immediately enter rich woods on a boardwalk.

0.3 Meet the Big Cypress Loop. Veer left on this narrow single-track path. The Goldenrod Trail continues straight.

0.4 Reach a spur trail leading a short distance to a bottomland hardwood swamp and a 500-year-old bald cypress tree towering over the rest of the cypresses.

0.7 Rejoin the Goldenrod Trail on a wider track.

0.8 Reach another trail junction. Here the Goldenrod Trail makes an extra loop. Though you can keep forward and shortcut the loop, this hike stays left, going with the extra loop for maximum mileage. Circle a seasonal maple wetland centered by Buck Head Branch using a boardwalk and bridges. Come very close to noisy SR 202.

1.3 Turn right in row-cropped pines, northwesterly, as an unmarked trail keeps forward.

1.4 Complete the extra loop. Stay straight, still on the Goldenrod Trail.

1.5 Stay forward, joining the green-blazed Gopher Tortoise Ridge Trail. Shortly come near a man-made pond, then curve north in sandy pines and turkey oaks.

2.3 Intersect the Goldenrod Trail after an easterly turn. Keep forward, rejoining the Goldenrod Trail. Cross Sawmill Slough on boardwalks.

2.4 Meet Lake Oneida and the Blueberry Trail. Turn left here and begin circling around the north arm of the lake.

2.7 A spur trail leads left to UNF Drive.

2.8 Pass a bridge leading to an island in Lake Oneida. A picnic area is nearby, too. Keep straight along the lake, passing the UNF boat rental area.

3.0 Emerge at Parking Lot 100, near the Red Maple Boardwalk, completing the hike.

14 Castaway Island Preserve Walk

Enjoy a walk through 300 acres on the Intracoastal Waterway in an otherwise developed area of eastern Duval County
near Jacksonville Beach. Castaway Island Preserve offers
concrete paths and a long boardwalk, plus an observation
tower, to help you explore the human and natural history of
this nexus of land and sea.

Distance: 1.7 miles
Approximate hiking time: 1 to
1.5 hours
Difficulty: Easy
Trail surface: Concrete and
boardwalk
Best season: Oct through Apr
Other trail users: None
Canine compatibility: Leashed
dogs permitted

Fees and permits: No fees or
permits required
Schedule: Sunrise to sunset
Maps: Castaway Island Preserve,
USGS Jacksonville Beach
Trail contacts: Castaway Island
Preserve, 2885 San Pablo Rd.,
Jacksonville, FL 32224; (904)
630-4100; www.coj.net

Finding the trailhead: From the Beach Boulevard exit on SR 9A
east of downtown, take Beach Boulevard east for 5 miles to San
Pablo Road and a traffic light. Turn left on San Pablo Road and follow it for 0.4 mile to the preserve entrance on your right. Be careful,
as the entrance is hard to spot until you are right up on it. Drive a
short distance into the preserve, parking just past the education center. GPS Trailhead Coordinates: N30° 17' 45.51", W81° 26' 3.30"

The Hike

Castaway Island Preserve is a jewel in the city of Jacksonville's parks system—and it was about as expensive as a dia-

mond. Situated along the west shoreline of the Intracoastal Waterway near San Pablo Creek, the 300-acre tract was the last tract of land available for park development between Atlantic and Beach boulevards. Castaway Island was purchased in the early 2000s for over $3 million, with several hundred thousand dollars used to develop the park facilities. And to think it was once a trailer park! (At one time Navy personnel were stationed here in a small community called Pablo Palms, complete with trailers and a swimming pool.) The amenities these days focus on what nature offers—an attractive woodland enveloped by marsh and tidal creeks.

The preserve was opened in 2004 and quickly became a favorite among locals for its access to walking trails, picnicking, or launching a canoe or kayak from a small boat basin into San Pablo Creek, part of the Intracoastal Waterway which connects to the St. Johns River. Castaway Island Preserve is but one tract in a greater whole, designed to safeguard nature's best. The Preservation Project Jacksonville (PPJ) has acquired over 50,000 acres of land to help preserve wild northeast Florida, offer recreation places and open spaces, and to keep the quality of life high on the First Coast.

The trail system is great for kids as it offers loads of fun interpretive information, delivered as if it were from the "survivors on Castaway Island"—critters such as raccoons and armadillos. The hike leaves the picnic area, traveling along the park road before turning north to explore the interpretive nature path known as the Island Trail.

Marsh borders the land berm on which you travel, giving the walk an airy, open feel. Shorebirds may be in the nearby waters. You will certainly see them at the canoe/

kayak launch if nowhere else. The Island Trail has short spurs leading to the interpretive stations. Take the elevated boardwalk extending easterly into the marsh. A labyrinth of tidal creeks snakes through the marsh grasses. These wetlands are important not only for the "survivors on Castaway Island," but also for all of Jacksonville. These wetlands help absorb waters in floods and storms but also filter pollutants from the water and provide important aquifer recharge areas. The boardwalk extends a full 0.2 mile toward Pablo Creek. A boardwalk this long is not cheap. Get your money's worth by checking out both elevated viewing areas. The Beach Boulevard Bridge arches over the Intracoastal Waterway. Houses rise on the far side of the marsh— the likely fate for this area if it were not for Preservation Project Jacksonville.

To get your full exercise value out of Castaway Island you must take every trail. This means walking the boardwalk to the canoe/kayak launch and also walking up to the covered observation tower located near the end of the main park road. Finally, pick up the concrete path leading toward San Pablo Road. This trail wanders by the picnic area, past a butterfly garden, and ends at the road next to an ancient double-trunked cedar that easily predates the state of Florida.

Miles and Directions

0.0 Pick up the concrete path in the picnic area across the park road from the education center. Begin walking toward the Intracoastal Waterway. Cedars, palms, and wax myrtle border the trail. Turn left and join the Island Trail.

0.3 The preserve boardwalk leads right. Keep forward, walking to the Island Trail's end, which forms a small loop, then return to the boardwalk.

Castaway Island Preserve Walk

San Pablo Creek

Dock and Canoe Launch

Observation Platform

Island Trail

PRESERVE

CASTAWAY ISLAND

P 14

Education Center

Butterfly Garden

Huge Cedar Tree

San Pablo Road

N

Kilometer 0.1

Mile 0.1

0.4 Begin walking the boardwalk toward San Pablo Creek and the Intracoastal Waterway. Enjoy great views of the tidal marsh from the elevated walkway.

0.6 Reach the east end of the boardwalk. Enjoy views from two elevated overlooks, then backtrack to the main park road.

0.9 After reaching the main park road, walk toward the Intracoastal Waterway and take the boardwalk leading over the water and to a canoe/kayak launch. The small basin was dug to help keep water here so paddlers could access San Pablo Creek. Also, walk up the shaded observation tower for another marsh view. Look north to spot the boardwalk you were on earlier. Now, pick up the concrete path heading toward San Pablo Road.

1.3 Pass the picnic area, trailhead, and education center, still heading toward San Pablo Road. Look for winged creatures in the butterfly garden.

1.5 Reach the park gate and San Pablo Road. Note the ancient double-trunked cedar tree. Backtrack.

1.7 Complete the hike.

15 Fort George Island Trail

Make a loop on the grounds of an old club, now a superlative natural getaway with a sea view, hills, lush woods, and the unique opportunity to walk portions of a former golf course now being reclaimed by Mother Nature.

Distance: 3.3-mile loop
Approximate hiking time: 1.5 to 2.5 hours
Difficulty: Moderate
Trail surface: Natural surfaces
Best season: Oct through Apr
Other trail users: Bicyclists
Canine compatibility: Leashed dogs permitted
Fees and permits: No fees or permits currently required
Schedule: 8 a.m. to sunset
Maps: Fort George Island Cultural State Park Multiuse Trail, USGS Mayport
Trail contacts: Talbot Islands State Parks, 12157 Heckscher Dr., Jacksonville, FL 32226; (904) 251-2320; www.Florida StateParks.org

Finding the trailhead: From SR 9A east of downtown, take Heckscher Drive 9.4 miles east to Fort George Road. Turn left on Fort George Road. At 0.5 mile, reach a split; stay right toward the Ribault Clubhouse. Travel a total of 1.9 miles from Heckscher Drive and reach a parking area on the far side of the road from the Ribault Club, near a historic marker indicating the site of the San Juan del Puerto Mission. GPS Trailhead Coordinates: N30° 25' 40.03", W81° 25' 33.29"

The Hike

This is a great hike in a historic setting near the mouth of the St. Johns River. As with other islands of the First Coast, what came to be known as Fort George Island was once occupied by the Timucuan Indians. They got their sustenance from the nearby estuaries, and left large shell mounds as evidence of their time here. When European powers set about conquering and controlling North America, the French entered these parts, and Jean Ribault claimed Fort George Island. Later, the Spaniards took over the island and established a Christian mission named San Juan del Puerto in 1587. Mission records detail life of the Timucuan, who soon succumbed to European diseases.

In the early 1700s England came to possess the island, naming it Fort George, and planned to use it as a base of operations to dislodge the Spanish from Florida. The European wranglings continued until the United States established Florida as an American territory in 1821. The island then entered its "club phase," when John Rollins established the Fort George Island Hotel in 1875, but a fire and yellow fever soon did it in.

Then, in the 1920s, the plush Ribault Club was opened. Its affluent members enjoyed a nine-hole golf course among other activities. Over time the Ribault Club lost its luster. The buildings and grounds were purchased by the state of Florida in 1989, which established Fort George Island Cultural State Park on the land. Today the refurbished Ribault Clubhouse offers an excellent meeting and retreat location, while the grounds now contain an underutilized hiking trail where you can enjoy maritime forests, as well as the unique experience of walking the holes of the old golf course. The park map shows the trail superimposed over the golf course holes, most of which can still be seen, although trees are now coming up on the fairways.

Highlights of the hike include Point Isabel, worth the extra walk as it overlooks the Fort George River, and Mount Cornelia, one of the highest places along the Florida coast. View other nearby islands from this vantage, and finally, enjoy some vertical variation near the hike's end, when you traverse Mount Cornelia. While here, check out the nearby Kingsley Plantation with its tabby ruins and watery views.

Miles and Directions

0.0 As you face the Ribault Clubhouse, look right across a grassy field for a brown hiker sign. Walk the field toward the sign, then enter a 4-foot-wide grass and sand path in the forest. Wander between forest and clearing.

0.6 The trail curves sharply back to the northeast, then passes through a picturesque live-oak cathedral.

1.2 Span a dug canal by culvert. The forest continues to subtly change from live oak to pine and every combination of the two.

1.6 Make a sharp left near an old golf hole. The trail heads north from there.

1.9 Meet the road leading to the Kingsley Plantation. Walk left about 50 feet along the road, picking up the trail on the north side of the road.

2.0 The trail splits. A shortcut heads right. Stay left, aiming for Point Isabel, crossing an open former fairway.

2.2 Take the spur trail leading straight for Point Isabel.

2.3 Reach Point Isabel. Follow concrete steps leading down to an old dock and a viewing point of the Fort George River and Big Talbot Island to the north and the dunes of Little Talbot Island to the east. Note the small beach along the river's edge to your left as you look out on the river. Backtrack.

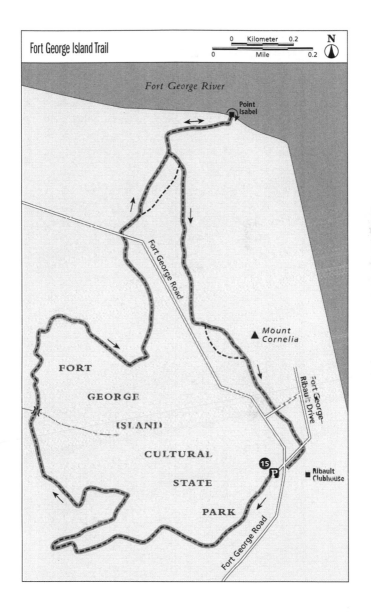

0   Kilometer   0.2

0   Mile   0.2

N

Fort George River

Point
Isabel

Fort George Road

▲ *Mount
Cornelia*

Fort George-
Ribault Drive

FORT

GEORGE

ISLAND

CULTURAL

STATE

PARK

15 P

■ Ribault
Clubhouse

Fort George Road

2.4 Rejoin the loop, now heading for the Ribault Club.

2.5 Keep straight past the shortcut trail intersection. Keep south amid more live oaks.

2.8 Bisect a closed sand road.

2.9 The trail splits. Keep straight, climbing over Mount Cornelia, while an easy route heads right. Note poured concrete on the path.

3.0 The easy route rejoins the main path.

3.2 Cross a park road.

3.3 Join a gravel road within sight of the Ribault Club. Turn right to reach the hiker parking area and complete the hike.

16 Nature Loop at Little Talbot Island

This easy day hike starts at the Little Talbot Island State Park campground, wandering along a tidal creek before entering rolling maritime hammock woodland. Since the hike is relatively short, consider adding many of the other available activities at the park to your walk, including, camping, biking, or beachcombing.

Distance: 0.8-mile loop

Approximate hiking time: 0.5 to 1 hour

Difficulty: Easy

Trail surface: Natural surfaces

Best season: Year-round

Other trail users: None

Canine compatibility: Leashed dogs permitted

Fees and permits: Entrance fee required

Schedule: 8 a.m. to sunset

Maps: Campground Nature Loop at Little Talbot Island, USGS Mayport

Trail contacts: Talbot Islands State Parks, 12157 Heckscher Dr., Jacksonville, FL 32226; (904) 251-2320; www.Florida StateParks.org

Finding the trailhead: From exit 358 on I-95 north of downtown, take FL 105 (Heckscher Drive) east for 22 miles to the state park entrance station. Be aware that after 20 miles, FL 105 turns into FL A1A. First, drive to the park entrance station on your right; get a trail map and day pass for the campground, as well as the combination to the campground gate; and then drive across A1A to the campground. Follow the signs for campsites #25–#40. Park near the campground boat ramp near campsite #34, then walk a short distance through the campground to campsite #39. The trail starts near campsite #39. GPS Trailhead Coordinates: N30° 27' 23.18", W81° 25' 15.72"

The Hike

Little Talbot Island State Park is part of the greater Talbot Islands State Parks. In addition to Little Talbot, there is Big Talbot Island, Long Island, Fort George Island, and Amelia Island State Recreation Area. Little Talbot has a forty-unit campground that serves as a well-placed base camp for exploring the beaches, marshlands, and the history of the tidal region, and is the starting point for this hike.

The campground is across A1A from the ocean and backs up to a salt marsh. The campground is divided into three loops of hard, packed lime rock set in an undulating maritime forest that makes for a scenic setting. A campground gate keeps the area safe and secure. You must get the gate combination to get to the hike!

The hike leaves the wooded campground on a narrow spit of land on a rolling sand path. The Myrtle Creek marsh stretches out to your right and is close enough that the path can be a little damp on a high tide. Ahead, a small beach opens on Myrtle Creek. Here you can walk toward the tidal stream as it pulses through the low salt grasses which avail far-reaching views to wooded lands lying west. You may see shorebirds in the area, too. Anglers are often seen casting for redfish and sea trout in the tidal estuary. The marsh is also great for crabbing.

Beyond Myrtle Creek, the trail enters heavy woods, situated on the same ancient dune line as the campground. A mixture of slash pine, live oak, gnarled red cedar, Southern magnolia, and palm rise from the soil-covered sands that once marked the edge of the Atlantic. An understory of American holly, saw palmetto, and yaupon add density to height. The sand-based trail overlain with forest duff offers periodic interpretive stops that explain the plants and animals of Little Talbot Island. Note the linear layout of the ancient dunes and how they parallel the shoreline of today. It is hard to imagine that this was once open shoreline. Barrier islands shift over time, and you may hear a roar on the hike. Amazingly, that is the sound of the Atlantic Ocean crashing on the shore of the island's east side. Little Talbot Island has more than 5 miles of pristine beach. Sunbathe, surf-cast, or just watch the waves roll in. Don't be surprised to see surfers riding the waves out on North Point. Consider biking the park's paved roads and trails. Beach cruisers are for rent at the state park office.

Big Talbot Island is even more on the quiet side. This is another sea island that offers several short nature trails, canoeing, fishing, and sunbathing. There is a spot known as the Bluffs with a view of Nassau Sound that photographers love. Amelia Island is next up the chain of Sea Islands. The state recreation area provides the opportunity to rent horses and saddle up for a ride along the beach. So even if this hike is relatively short, you can easily make a day of it—or night, too, if you stay in the campground—at Little Talbot Island.

Miles and Directions

0.0 Pick up the signed nature trail leaving near campsite #39 in the park campground. Travel south on a wide, sandy path.

0.1 Reach the loop portion of the hike in an open marsh. Keep right along Myrtle Creek. A spur path leads to a small beach on Myrtle Creek. At lower tides you will see exposed oyster bars.

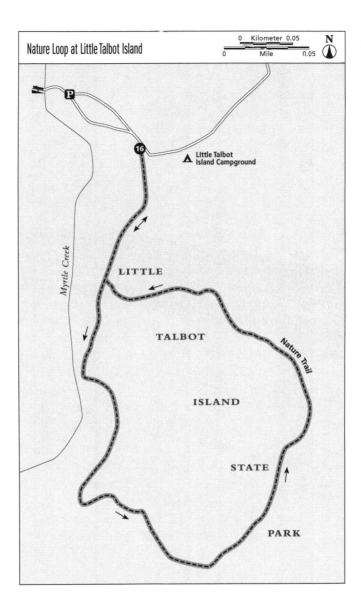

Nature Loop at Little Talbot Island

0   Kilometer   0.05
0   Mile   0.05

N

Myrtle Creek

LITTLE

TALBOT

ISLAND

STATE

PARK

Nature Trail

16

Little Talbot
Island Campground

P

0.2 Turn away from Myrtle Creek, entering maritime hammock. Live oaks with limbs covered in resurrection ferns stretch over the forest.

0.5 Briefly open onto an open sand dune area. The brightness contrasts with the deep forest of before. Undulate over some of the highest wooded dunes.

0.7 Finish the loop portion of the hike, leaving the maritime hammock and returning to Myrtle Creek.

0.8 Reach the campground, completing the hike.

17   Little Talbot Island Hiking Trail

Enjoy the best of Jacksonville's coastal islands on this hike. Start your trek near the Atlantic Ocean, then travel through rolling oceanside woodland before returning to the Atlantic. The rest of your hike is a sandy walk, where you travel along an unspoiled beach with good shelling opportunities.

Distance: 3.8-mile loop
Approximate hiking time: 2 to 2.5 hours
Difficulty: Moderate due to hills and potentially loose sand
Trail surface: Natural surfaces, a little asphalt
Best season: Oct through Apr
Other trail users: Bicyclists
Canine compatibility: Leashed dogs permitted on forested portion of the hike, prohibited on the beach
Fees and permits: Entrance fee required
Schedule: 8 a.m. to sunset
Maps: Little Talbot Island Hiking Trail, USGS Mayport
Trail contacts: Talbot Islands State Parks, 12157 Heckscher Dr., Jacksonville, FL 32226; (904) 251-2320; www.Florida StateParks.org

Finding the trailhead: From exit 358 on I-95 north of downtown, take FL 105 (Heckscher Drive) east for 22 miles to the state park entrance station. Be aware that after 20 miles, FL 105 turns into FL A1A. Drive past the park entrance station on your right, then continue to the north beach parking area. GPS Trailhead Coordinates: N30° 27' 30.8", W81° 24' 49.7"

The Hike

Little Talbot Island is one of the largest undeveloped barrier islands in Florida and is part of the greater Sea Islands. The vast St. Johns River forms a large estuarine system, north of which lie the Sea Islands, the set of barrier islands extending northward into Georgia and South Carolina. Long ago they were the home of the Timucuan Indians. Later, European explorers established rice and indigo plantations there. Then they were the sites of Florida's first resorts. Beyond the island beaches are enormous live oaks draped in Spanish moss lording over rich maritime hammocks, through which this hike travels. As the islands slope back down toward the mainland, tidal creeks rise and fall among the marshes. Time and nature move slowly here.

While seemingly every segment of Florida's coastline is being developed, preserves such as this state park offer not only a chance to explore this oceanside environment in its natural state, but also a chance to see the forces of nature at work, shaping the land—a place where water endlessly breaks against the shore and where winds sculpt the vegetation. Away from the shore you can see where the ceaseless winds and tides, along with the occasional major storm, have shifted the island itself. Barrier islands are always in a state of flux. On the north end of this hike the Atlantic is cutting into high dunes, slowly moving Little Talbot Island as surely as the moon creates the tides.

Make sure and bring a little bug dope for the woods and a hat and sunglasses for the beach part of the hike. After traveling through the open park entrance road, enter the relatively cool and dark world of the maritime hammock. Palms, cedar, Southern magnolia, slash pines, and the magnificent live oaks form a woodland cathedral. Yaupon and palmetto rise from the forest floor. Occasional open areas contrast with the thick woods. Although the trail surface is sand it is more stable than you think, since tree fodder and forest duff help stabilize it. However, areas that receive direct sunlight will have looser, dried-out sand. Expect an undulating trail that is never level for long and offers bona fide hills with drop-offs astride the trail that will surprise.

Occasional resting benches are situated along the path. The path is marked with occasional hiker/biker symbols and arrows pointing you in the right direction. However, the wide trail bordered by thick woods leaves an easily followable route. Continue north in the remote heart of the island. Enjoy this slice of wild Florida before turning toward the Atlantic near the north end of Little Talbot Island. Leave the hammock and wind through dune swales topped with windswept vegetation. Stay on the trail and off the fragile dunes.

Your southbound walk along the Atlantic Ocean reveals the state of natural beaches. Craggy cedars and palms have fallen into the sands. Shells will be embedded at your feet. Ocean fodder and other vegetation will be lying on the beach, very different from the contrived, sterile, raked beaches of resorts.

Depending on the tides, make your own route along the sandy shore. Eventually the state park beach–access boardwalk will come into view. Reach the boardwalk, then travel over low windswept dunes and come to the parking area, where a picnic pavilion, restrooms, and cold outdoor showers await.

Miles and Directions

0.0 From the north parking area near the beach, take the dedicated asphalt hike/bike path running parallel with the park entrance road back toward FL A1A.

0.2 Pass the park entrance station. Continue on the asphalt path.

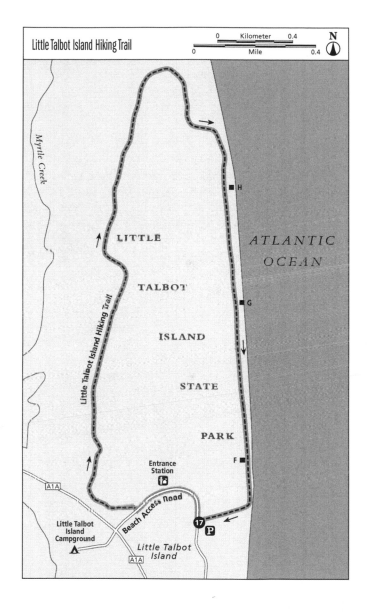

Little Talbot Island Hiking Trail

0 Kilometer 0.4
0 Mile 0.4

N

Myrtle Creek

LITTLE

TALBOT

ISLAND

STATE

PARK

ATLANTIC OCEAN

Little Talbot Island Hiking Trail

H

G

F

Entrance Station

A1A

Little Talbot Island Campground

Beach Access Road

17 P

Little Talbot Island

A1A

0.3 Cross the park entrance road to enter full-fledged woods on a natural-surface trail. There is no parking allowed on the park entrance road at the trail's actual beginning. Pass a trailside kiosk and begin your woodland journey.

0.4 Come near FL A1A (Heckscher Drive) before turning north and running along a hilly dune line parallel with the Atlantic Ocean.

2.0 The trail curves northeasterly toward the Atlantic Ocean. Slice between big dunes as the ocean roar rises.

2.5 Reach the Atlantic Ocean in an area where dunes drop straight to the water and have been cut by the waves. Turn right, southbound, with the Atlantic Ocean to your left and land to your right. At high tide you may have to walk through the water a bit to get around the high dunes, which soon give way to a more-sloping beach, with ample sands for walking no matter the tides.

2.7 Pass beach marker H.

3.1 Pass beach marker G.

3.6 Pass beach marker F.

3.7 Reach the boardwalk, turn right, and cross low dunes.

3.8 Complete the hike, returning to the north parking area.

18 Pumpkin Hill Creek Preserve Hike

This newer Florida state park offers an evolving trail system through a variety of plant communities. This hike traces double-track paths through rare oak scrub, pine flatwoods, maritime hammock, and along tidal Pumpkin Hill Creek with its extensive marshes.

Distance: 2.1-mile loop with spurs
Approximate hiking time: 1 to 2 hours
Difficulty: Easy
Trail surface: Natural surfaces
Best season: Oct through Apr
Other trail users: Bicyclists and equestrians
Canine compatibility: Leashed dogs permitted

Fees and permits: No fees or permits required
Schedule: 8 a.m. to sunset
Maps: Pumpkin Hill Creek Preserve State Park, USGS Mayport
Trail contacts: Pumpkin Hill Creek Preserve State Park, 13802 Pumpkin Hill Rd., Jacksonville, Fl 32226; (904) 696-5980; www.FloridaStateParks.org

Finding the trailhead: From SR 9A east of downtown, take Heckscher Drive a short distance east to New Berlin Road. Turn left on New Berlin Road and follow it for 3.7 miles to Cedar Point Road. Turn right on Cedar Point Road and follow it for 4.6 miles to Pumpkin Hill Road. Turn left on Pumpkin Hill Road and follow it for 0.8 mile to turn left into the trailhead parking area. GPS Trailhead Coordinates: N30° 28' 25.2", W81° 29' 14.0"

The Hike

Pumpkin Hill Creek, in the far northeastern reaches of Duval County, used to be the back of beyond, but the tentacles of Jacksonville have been stretching that way. Ironically, with more people you need more green spaces;

thus, the St. Johns River Water Management District, the city of Jacksonville, and the state of Florida pooled their money to purchase nearly 4,000 acres along the west shore of Pumpkin Hill Creek, a tidal marsh stream. The land has undergone many uses. Long ago, vast stands of old-growth slash pine were turpentined. The sap from the evergreens was collected when men made an incision in the bark and installed a V-shaped metal plate, which helped pine sap drain into a pottery-type cup. The sap was then distilled into rosin and turpentine. A new slit was made each year in the trees, just a little lower than the year before, creating what was known as a "cat face." Later, the same trees were cut down for wood when the area was timbered. Still later, the land became a private hunting preserve, and oysters were processed at a location on Pumpkin Hill Creek.

Today, Pumpkin Hill Creek Preserve is a large wildland where you can hear the wind blow through the pines, see songbirds jumping from branch to branch in oak scrub, watch deer browse beneath a live oak, or paddle your canoe/kayak along the open marshes. Land managers are working hard to restore the native plants and animals to the area. Fire is an important component of the habitat restoration. The numerous sand roads on the tract are effective divisions used to manage the preserve.

Since the park is new, the trail system is still evolving. Currently it follows already-established fire roads, but as the preserve grows in popularity, the park will respond to the demand for the most scenic trails possible. Expect reroutes and new trails leading to natural highlights on the property. This hike already travels to two vistas overlooking Pumpkin Hill Creek; however, be apprised that the trail system may change between visits.

The trail system uses color-coded paths. This hike makes a loop with the Blue Trail, then takes the Green Trail out to Pumpkin Hill Creek. The hike immediately enters its signature environment—flatwoods scrub. The scrub oak trees that grow here are important bird habitats. Oak scrub is one of the most endangered habitats in Florida because it is so easily developed and little of it remains. Widely scattered pines rise above the low canopy. Ahead, the oak scrub gives way to palmetto prairie pocked with pines.

The hike turns north and then east. A spur trail leads to Pumpkin Hill Creek, where you can relax under live oaks while looking over the tidal stream bordered in marsh grasses. The Blue Trail carries you back to the trailhead, but you're not done yet. Head east on the Green Trail to reach a second overlook of Pumpkin Hill Creek. The tidal stream flows through a wide expanse of marsh grasses bordered by woodland on the far side. Anglers or paddlers may be seen here. Backtrack to the trailhead. On your next visit try some different trails; you may even have some new ones to hike.

Miles and Directions

0.0   Leave the large parking area and pass around a pole gate to head westerly into low oak scrub. The park office is visible to your left. Travel a sandy double-track. The Blue Trail, Red Trail, Yellow Trail, and Purple Trail all run in conjunction.

0.3   Reach a trail junction. Here, the Blue Trail turns acutely right while the other trails keep forward, then split just ahead near a wooden gazebo. Begin traveling northeast in pine flatwoods.

0.5   A closed road comes in from the left.

0.8   The Blue Trail turns right at a signed junction while sand roads keep forward. Now travel easterly toward Pumpkin Hill Road.

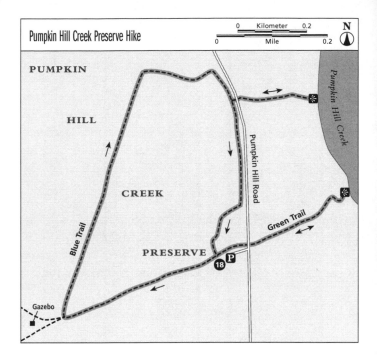

Pumpkin Hill Creek Preserve Hike

0.9 Meet Pumpkin Hill Road. Turn right on a fire line, then reach a gate and cross Pumpkin Hill Road. Take the spur path heading easterly.

1.1 Reach Pumpkin Hill Creek in a live-oak copse. This is a scenic shaded area ideal for stopping. Backtrack and cross Pumpkin Hill Road, resuming a southerly track along a fence line before curving away from it.

1.5 Reach the parking area. Take the park entrance road east; cross Pumpkin Hill Road, then join the Green Trail.

1.8 Come to the second overlook of Pumpkin Hill Creek. Backtrack to the trailhead.

2.1 Complete the hike.

19 Willow Nature Trail

This short trek wanders through a combination of wooded island swamp and hilly maritime hammock forest at Fort Clinch State Park. This state park on Florida's northernmost barrier island also offers plenty of other activities to round out your experience, including a tour of the historic fort.

Distance: 0.8-mile double loop
Approximate hiking time: 0.5 to 1 hour
Difficulty: Easy
Trail surface: Natural surfaces
Best season: Year-round
Other trail users: None
Canine compatibility: Leashed dogs permitted

Fees and permits: Entrance fee required
Schedule: 8 a.m. to sunset
Maps: Fort Clinch State Park, USGS Fernandina Beach
Trail contacts: Fort Clinch State Park, 2601 Atlantic Ave., Fernandina Beach, FL 32034; (904) 277-7274; www.FloridaState Parks.org

Finding the trailhead: From exit 373 on I-95 north of Jacksonville, take SR A1A 16 miles easterly to the town of Fernandina Beach. Once in town, A1A becomes 8th Street. Stay on 8th Street to meet Atlantic Avenue. Turn right on Atlantic Avenue and follow it for 2 miles to reach the state park, on your left. Enter the state park and stay with the main road for 2.2 miles; the trailhead will be on your left. GPS Trailhead Coordinates: N30° 41' 54.17", W81° 26' 36.78"

The Hike

This hike is comprised of several interconnected nature trails meandering through wooded dunes and along a wetland. The hike begins in wooded dunes. Live oak, palm,

Southern magnolia, and holly thrive above an understory of yaupon and palmetto. Spanish moss covers anything that doesn't move. Ferns gain purchase in the fertile soil. You soon dip to a series of ponds, dug when the Civilian Conservation Corps (CCC) developed the park in the 1930s—not to retain water, but simply to acquire fill to elevate the park roadway. At this point, the hike travels elevated berms between the ponds, enveloped in vegetation. The hike climbs back into ancient wooded dunes before returning to the ponds one last time. A little bit of trail re-walking returns you to the hike's beginning.

Fort Clinch began to take shape in 1842, long before the CCC days, when the U.S. purchased the north end of Amelia Island for a military installation as part of a program to protect our country's seaports. Fort Clinch was only partially completed by Civil War times, which is why different-colored bricks were used in its construction. The first bricks came from Georgia, but shipments stopped after the conflict. The top bricks came from New York. The Confederates were first in possession of the fort during wartime, but then the Union captured several forts up the coast, leaving Fort Clinch isolated, so the Confederates abandoned it.

Construction was renewed after the Yankees took over, but was not completed even after war's end. The fort was then deactivated until the Spanish-American War in 1898. The bastion soon resumed its slow deterioration. The fort was used once more during World War II as a Coast Guard surveillance post. By this time it had passed from the federal government to private hands, and then to the state of Florida. In the state's hands Fort Clinch became one of Florida's first state parks, further developed by the CCC during the Great Depression. It has been well taken care of ever since.

Today, you can visit a restored brick Civil War fort; camp in either of two appealing yet diverse campgrounds; and enjoy three types of marine environments—the Atlantic Ocean, Cumberland Sound, and the Amelia River. Nearly a mile of beachfront looks out over the Atlantic Ocean. The sand is tan and gently sloping, and sunbathers and swimmers cool off in the waves. A jetty, first built during the Spanish-American War in 1898 and since rebuilt, extends over a mile into the Atlantic. This makes the sand extend out in a point before turning beyond the jetty. Ocean lovers and anglers enjoy a 2,000 foot pier along the jetty.

Take the time to tour Fort Clinch, which includes visits to the jail, officers' quarters, courtyard, and the cannons. Time your hike to see the fort come alive during a reenactment. These take place during the first weekend of every month and on special occasions. Rangers and volunteers dress in costume from the 1860s and portray life as it was during this time, going about their chores. They will be happy to answer your questions about what they are up to, but they know nothing of life after the 1860s. If you miss one of these events, tour the fort anyway; the views from the top are spectacular!

Miles and Directions

0.0 With your back to Fort Clinch Road, you will see four trails entering the woods. Take the second trail to your left, not the Fort Clinch Bicycle Trail, which is the trail farthest to your left. Join a single-track path descending in a rich maritime hammock forest. Shortly reach several small, moss-covered dug ponds bordered with willow trees. These willows give the nature trail its name. The trail then picks up a berm lying between these ponds.

Willow Nature Trail

Fort Clinch Road

Fort Clinch Bicycle Trail

Fort Clinch Bicycle Trail

Willow Nature Trail

FORT CLINCH

STATE PARK

N

Kilometer 0.05

0

0 0.05

Mile

P

19

0.1 Make a trail junction. Stay left, as a high-water bypass stays right. Continue on a level berm between old dug ponds.

0.3 Bridge an old pond. Climb back into maritime hammock forest in rolling terrain.

0.4 Reach a trail junction. Here, a path leads left back to the trailhead. Stay right on the Willow Trail, wandering back to the ponds.

0.6 Reach the High-Water Bypass. Stay left and soon meet the trail you were on before. Backtrack to the trailhead.

0.8 Complete the hike.

20 Fort Clinch Bicycle Trail

Don't be discouraged by the word bicycle in this trail's name. The scenic path is open to hikers and is one of the better treks in the Jacksonville sphere. The hike travels a slender but long loop through maritime hardwood hammock forest on (nearly) continuously undulating terrain.

Distance: 6-mile loop
Approximate hiking time: 3 to 3.5 hours
Difficulty: More challenging due to hills and distance
Trail surface: Natural surfaces, a little road walking
Best season: Oct through Apr
Other trail users: Bicyclists and runners
Canine compatibility: Leashed dogs permitted
Fees and permits: Entrance fee required
Schedule: 8 a.m. to sunset
Maps: Fort Clinch State Park, USGS Fernandina Beach
Trail contacts: Fort Clinch State Park, 2601 Atlantic Ave., Fernandina Beach, FL 32034; (904) 277-7274; www.FloridaState Parks.org

Finding the trailhead: From exit 373 on I-95 north of Jacksonville, take SR A1A 16 miles easterly to the town of Fernandina Beach. Once in town A1A becomes 8th Street. Stay on 8th Street to meet Atlantic Avenue. Turn right on Atlantic Avenue and follow it for 2 miles to reach the state park, on your left. Enter the state park and stay with the main road for 3.3 miles to the Fort Clinch parking area. Pick up the trail on the east side of the entrance road just before you reach the main parking area. GPS Trailhead Coordinates: N30° 42' 12.87", W81° 27' 10.26"

The Hike

This is a great hike. Located within the confines of Fort Clinch State Park, this trail leaves historic Fort Clinch—which you should visit either before or after this hike—and then heads south along a wooded dune line running through the heart of Amelia Island. The ups and downs are almost constant as the path crests these tree-covered dunes and then dips into swales, only to repeat the performance again and again. You finally reach the southernmost point of the trail, cross Fort Clinch Road, and curve back north. At this point the trail travels along Egan's Creek, a tidal stream bordered by a vast swath of marsh grasses. This section is decidedly less hilly but does have sections of forested dunes, including one particularly high dune that offers a far-reaching vista to the west beyond the marshes of Egan's Creek.

Before becoming intimidated, realize that the majority of trail undulations are less than 20 feet up or down. It is the continuous nature of them that will test your mettle. Occasionally, the trail is forced to the road due to extremely sloping or wet terrain. These road walks are very short, however, but do provide you a means of shortcutting the loop should you choose not to do the entire 6 miles. Simply look across the road and you should be able to pick up the northbound section of the trail fairly easily. Bicyclists do use the trail, but they are asked by the state park to pedal in a counterclockwise direction. Therefore, it is in your best interest to hike this loop in a clockwise direction; that way, you will see and hear any oncoming bicyclists.

Upon leaving Fort Clinch the path enters verdant woodland of live oak, cedar, dahoon holly, palm, palmetto, and yaupon. The ups and downs are immediate and unremitting. Not all these undulations are the result of old dunes becoming forested; when the Civilian Conservation Corps developed this park, they dug many channels in an effort to rid the area of standing water and thus mosquitoes. They didn't realize that such ditches would eventually fill with soil and plant duff, rendering them useless. Now the trail crosses these occasional dug channels.

The sandy track can be very rooty in places, so watch your footing. Generally speaking, the sand path isn't too loose; because it is mixed with plant duff and is mostly shaded, it doesn't dry out easily. The hiking eases on the northbound track. Egan's Creek is plainly visible through the trees. Expect more climbs and descents, but you will be accustomed to these by hike's end.

Miles and Directions

0.0 Leave the Fort Clinch parking area and walk just a few feet back down Fort Clinch Road. Look left for a single-track footpath leaving the northeast side of the road, traveling the loop in a clockwise direction. Do not take the section of the bike trail leaving directly from the Fort Clinch parking area, as you will be going in a counterclockwise direction, which the state park discourages.

0.2 Pass a pair of live oaks with huge bases and widespread arms.

0.4 Saddle alongside a high wooded dune that forces the trail very close to the road.

0.8 Come near a brick oil storage tank left over from the early days of Fort Clinch. The oil was used to illuminate the fort lighthouses. The Willow Nature Trail trailhead is just across the road.

1.0 Pass under a small transmission line. Continue south-easterly.

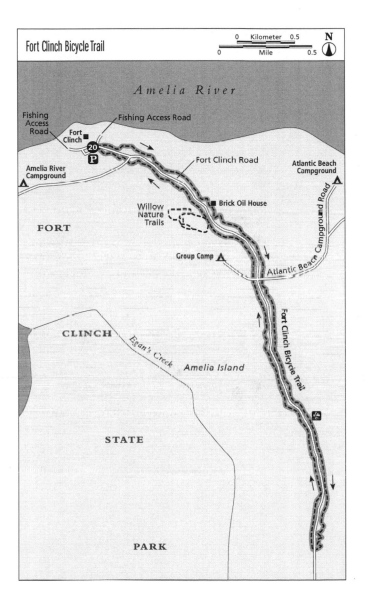

1.3 Cross the access road to the Atlantic Beach Campground. Come near dug canals.

1.9 Cross a tidal streamlet near the Fort Clinch Road bridge. Continue in forest.

2.3 Join Fort Clinch Road after slicing between wooded dunes.

2.4 Leave the road, reentering forest. Shortly rejoin the road.

2.5 Leave the road again, entering maritime woods.

3.0 Cross Fort Clinch Road. This is technically the trail's beginning but offers no parking. Turn northbound, with Egan's Creek to the west through the trees.

3.7 Climb a high dune with a good marsh vista.

3.9 Travel through an extended wetland.

4.1 Cross a tidal streamlet near the Fort Clinch Road bridge. Keep north.

4.7 Cross a sand service road leading to the park's group camp.

5.1 Bisect the Willow Nature Trail parking area. Stay with the trail closest to Fort Clinch Road.

5.8 Cross the road leading to Amelia River campground.

6.0 Emerge onto Fort Clinch parking area, completing the hike.